MIXOLOGIST

THE JOURNAL OF THE EUROPEAN COCKTAIL

VOLUME 3

PUBLISHER

JARED BROWN

EDITOR

ANISTATIA MILLER

CONTRIBUTORS

JARED BROWN, LYNN BRYON, SALVATORE CALABRESE,

DOMENICO CONSTANZO, PHILIP DUFF, ALBERTO GOMEZ FONT, STEFAN GABÁNY,

CAIRBRY HILL, SUE LECKIE, ANISTATIA MILLER, ALBERT MONTSERRAT,

GARY REGAN

MIXELLANY

Mixellany books may be purchased for educational, business, or sales promotional use. For information, please write to Mixellany Limited, 13 Bonchurch Road, West Ealing, London W13 9JE United Kingdom or email jared@mixellany.com

First edition

ISBN: 978-1-907434-00-6

British Library Cataloguing in Publication Data.
A catalogue record for this book is available from the British Library.

CONTENTS

WHAT'S IN THE BOTTLE

AND OTHER THINGS

From the Editor

I t has been three years and many thousands of miles since the last time we visited the Cocktail and spirits world with you. Our move to the UK, in 2007, has given us a new perspective on the bartending profession and its practitioners. Ever since this noble trade was born, mixologists and the people who write about them have scoured the world in search of new experiences, superior ingredients, and timeless flavours. It is time for *Mixologist* to look at the world outside the United States to see how drinks developed from a European perspective.

In this volume, the third, of *Mixologist: The Journal of the European Cocktail*, our intrepid travelling cocktailians take us a tour of the path of the bartender as seen through the eyes of cocktail guru Gary Regan. Sue Leckie details why the legendary master Peter Dorelli is such an inspired and inspirational spirit. Albert Montserrat pays tribute to his mentor and her father, Doña Maria Dolores and Miguel Boadas.

A replete charmer in his own right, Phil Duff discloses some the essential secrets of cultivating bartender-right charm. The histories of two highly-regarded guilds, the UKBG and the IBA, are presented by Lynn Byron and Domenico Constanzo, respectively. Too often overlooked by young bartenders today, these organizations were champions of the profession during its most embattled decades, and continue to press the cause.

Maestro Salvatore Calabrese sets the record straight about the crystal-clear, potent Dukes Martini. Sue Leckie returns to challenge the notion that all of Britain's best bars and bartenders reside in London.

A century of German bar culture is eloquently presented by Stefan Gabány. And as a finale, a century of Spanish cocktails is presented with all the passion and ecstasy of a true aficionado, by Alberto Gomez Font.

Naturally, we had to put in our two pence. This time, we uncover a few surprises in the origins and bloodline of the world's favourite morning pick-me-up, the Bloody Mary. And we take you through the halls and the history of Exposition Universelle des Vins et Spiritueux a place that is very near and dear to our hearts.

We hope you enjoy your Grand Tour of Europe in this Cocktail Continentale.

Classic Cocktails

An Investigation

THE BLOODY MARY & HER BLOODLINE

BY ANISTATIA MILLER & JARED BROWN

The **fights are endless** over the Bloody Mary. Was it a hangover cure created by an American entertainer visiting in Palm Beach, Florida? Was it a final toast crafted and named in a Parisian bar? Or something else?

Our story begins with the tomato. Tomato juice in particular. It's no surprise that barman Fernand "Pete" Petiot would have heard about this phenomenon. Born on 18 February 1900 in Paris where tomatoes had been used in cooking since the 1730s, he would have been more familiar with them than the average American.

Tomato juice was on French menus and ordered as early as 1914. It was available when Petiot took a job, in 1920, at the New York Bar: three years before it became Harry MacElhone's New York Bar.

Then the vodka arrived the same year. This is where the bloodline fight associated with the Bloody Mary's birth begins.

Who's Vodka Was It Anyway?

Purveyor to the Romanov Tsar Alexander III, Piotr A Smirnov had built a remark-
ably successful vodka distillery, beginning in the
1860s and capturing over half of the Moscow market within two
decades. He died in 1898 and his widow passed away the following year, leaving five sons to run the enterprise until 1902, when
Sergei and Alexey sold their interests, leaving Piotr, Nikolai, and
Vladimir to continue operations. Two years later, Piotr became
the sole owner when the remaining brothers released their rights
and interests in the family trademarks. The distillery continued
successful operations until the 1917 October Revolution.

According to an Opinion of the Court document filed in the
US Court of Appeals for the Third Circuit in September 2000
in a case against UDV North America and the Pierre Smirnoff
Company, Lwów. when Piotr died in 1910, his wife, Eugenia,
became the sole owner of the trade house. She operated the trade
house successfully until 1917. Historian Valerian Sergeevich
Obolensky, author of the 1993 online book *Russians in Exile: The
History of a Diaspora*, states that the distillery was confiscated on
22 November 1917 and was placed under state control.

It appears that Eugenia married an Italian diplomat and fled
to Italy before that fateful day, in all probability knowing that
the fall of the Tsarist Empire signalled personal disaster. She

eventually settled with her husband in Nice. She was not the only Smirnoff to emigrate to France.

Obolensky's account states that at the dawn of the revolution, Vladimir Smirnov was also in flight, hiding out in the Ukraine for a short time before he was arrested for being in cahoots with the tsarist regime and the White Army. He was given a death sentence by the Bolsheviks and was stood before a firing squad four times just to terrorize him. He finally escaped his captors, on 18 February 1918, with the aid of White Army forces.

This is where the facts get murky. Obolensky then places Smirnoff in Paris where, according to his research, this family member purchased a distillery on 2 May. But supporting evidence of this claim such as the location of his operation has not be discovered as of this publication.

However, the Opinion of the Court document states that Vladimir relocated to Constantinople (now Istanbul), where in 1920, he established a distillery under the title "Supplier to the Imperial Russian Court, Pierre Smirnoff Sons." Considering that few aristocratic Russians settled in Turkey but many made their way to France, it would be no surprise if the enterprising Vladimir exported his product to Paris.

He moved to Lvov, Poland, in 1924, where he opened another distillery. He opened yet another in Paris a year later under the name "Ste Pierre Smirnoff Fils" or "The Company of the Sons of Peter Smirnoff." He then changed the spelling of his family name from Smirnov to Smirnoff, as it was the popularly accepted spelling in French at that time.

His sister Eugenia first learned of Vladimir's use of the Smirnoff name and marks when the Parisian distillery was opened. She was upset that Vladimir had reneged on his bought agreement with his late brother and consequently herself. But with the documentary proof left behind in now-Communist-controlled Russia, she was unable to prove her claim. Vladimir continued his operations without restraint.

Roy Barton & the Bucket of Blood

While **Smirnov** was hawking his vodka around Paris, it was inevitable that he would stop at the New York Bar where the young Ferdnand "Pete" Petiot worked. There were a dozen or so cocktail bars in the Opéra district surrounding Rue Danou and Rue de Volney. Henry's, the Chatham Bar, but it was Tod Sloane's place, the New York Bar, where Smirnoff found a mixologist who was willing to play with this ethnic spirit.

In a January 1972 interview with *The Cleveland Press* reporter Al Thompson, Petiot explained that the first two customers to try his creation "were from Chicago, and they say there is a bar there named the Bucket of Blood. And there is a waitress there everybody calls Bloody Mary. One of the boys said that the drink reminds him of Bloody Mary, and the name stuck."

A similar story mentioned one of the customers by name. In Petiot's obituary which appeared in the 8 January 1975 edition of the *San Francisco Chronicle*, it states that: "Petiot was said to have been experimenting with vodka after having been introduced to it in Paris in 1920. He settled on a mix of half vodka and half tomato juice then introduced the drink where he worked at Harry's New York Bar which was frequented by American newspaper correspondents and bankers. An American entertainer Roy Barton, provided the name, saying it reminded him of a Chicago club, the Bucket of Blood."

Who was this entertainer named Roy Barton? He is listed as the composer of "Alabama Shuffle", "American Rag", and a few other ragtime compositions from the genre's 1920s heyday in New Orleans' infamous Storyville district. Born in the Big Easy, jazz and especially ragtime flourished amid the clubs and bars that sprung up between the licensed brothels frequented by tourists and naval personnel on leave after the district emerged in 1897. The city's leaders had studied the legalized red light districts in the European ports of Amsterdam and Hamburg to understand how to monitor and regulate prostitution, and they did so until the federal government shut down the operation in 1917, fearing that enlistees headed overseas to fight in the First World War would lose their innocence in Storyville's dens of iniquity.

When Storyille closed down, many jazz musicians headed north to St Louis and to Chicago. Ragtime hangouts sprung up in Chicago's most infamous vice district, the Levee, which formed in 1893 during the World Columbian Exposition and was situated on the city's Near South Side. The Bucket of Blood Saloon was one of the most famous. Situated at 19th and Federal Street, close to the high-class brothel, the Everleigh Club, made famous in Karen Abbott's 2007 book *Sin in the Second City: Madams, Ministers, Playboys, and the Battle for America's Soul*, the club remained a haven for jazz musicians and aficionados until, in the 1920s, the neighbourhood was slowly demolished.

Certainly Barton played at the Bucket of Blood. And it wouldn't be surprising for him to have fondly remembered a young waitress who had worked there as he sipped a farewell toast to his past with Petiot's creation.

But a future French classic doesn't easily become an international staple without help.

Tomato Juice Was Spiced Long Before The Bloody

The essential Bloody Mary formula—tomato juice, Worcestershire sauce, lemon juice, horseradish, Tabasco sauce, other hot sauces, salt, and pepper—had been around since the 19th century, but it was a virgin birth. *The Medical Record*, March 12, 1892 (William

Wood & Company, New York) printed this excerpt from London's *Hospital Gazette*:

> *A Recipe Returned from Over Sea.—It is reported that at the Manhattan Club in New York a warm beverage, called an "oyster cocktail," is largely dispensed. For the benefit of those who may be possessed of suicidal intentions, I give the recipe. Seven small oysters are dropped into a tumbler, to which must be added a pinch of salt, three drops of fiery Tobasco sauce, three drops of Mexican Chili pepper sauce, and a spoonful of lemon juice. To this mixture add a little horseradish and green pepper sauce, African pepper ketchup, black pepper, and fill up with tomato juice. This should be stirred with a spoon, very slightly crushing the oysters, which are then lifted out and eaten, the liquid following as a cocktail.*

According to the *Milwaukee Journal* in 1892, the recipe was slow to catch on in Britain. Due to a misunderstanding, perhaps from the misspelling of Tabasco above, people thought the recipe called for tobacco sauce. Tabasco, invented in 1868, was only twenty-four years old at this time.

In The Can

When the **French Lick Springs Hotel** resort in Indiana ran out of orange juice one day, in 1917, its French chef, Louis Perrin offered guests tomato juice. It was an immediate hit. Within three years, a handful of companies launched into commercial production. But canned tomato juice did not take off in the US until Chicago hotelier Ernest Byfield tasted his first glass of tomato juice cocktail, in 1927, while visiting the Yellow Cab Company owner, John Hertz, at his Miami vacation home.

Heir to a handful of luxury hotels including the Ambassador East as well as the College Inn Food Products Company, Byfield put his chefs to work on developing a "spiced" formula that included lemon juice and celery. It sold 60,000 cases in the first few months, strictly by word of mouth promotion amongst his cast of A-list friends and patrons.

It took a few years for the Bloody Mary's main ingredients and originator to meet on American soil.

Two years after Harry MacElhone took ownership of the New York Bar, Petiot moved, in 1925, to US in the midst of Prohibition. During a trip to Canton, Ohio, he met his future bride and was married.

Some sources say that Petiot then headed to the Savoy in London. But there is little evidence of this fact at time of this publication. What is known is that when the repeal bells rang out, the owner of the St Regis Hotel in New York, Mrs Mary Duke Biddle, convinced him to relocate, in 1934, and take a post under the Maxfield Parrish mural that adorned the hotel's King Cole Bar, heading up a staff of seventeen barmen. (The mural had been commissioned, in 1905, by her grandfather Nicholas Biddle as a gift to the hotel's original owner John Jacob Astor IV to hang in another of his properties, the Knickerbocker Hotel. When Astor died in 1912, his son Vincent sold the property to Benjamin Duke.)

The year before all of this happened, American businessman (an Ukrainian emigree) Rudolph Kunett purchased the rights from Vladimir Smirnoff to commercially produce vodka in the United States. With the establishment of Ste Pierre Smirnoff Fls, Inc by Kunnett plus Benjamin B McAlpin, Jr, Donald M McAlpin, and Townsend M McAlpin, vodka was available in New York just in time for Petiot's arrival.

Petiot's tomato creation went on the bar menu as the Red Snapper. Somewhere between its invention and its emigration to the New York, Worcestershire sauce had been added to his mix. But the drink didn't click with customers. Tomatoes grown on French soil are sweeter than their American cousins. Petiot hyped up his original recipe with salt, lemon juice, and Tabasco sauce, possibly from the old Oyster Cocktail recipe, then reinstituted Barton's name for the drink.

Bloody Mary got the attention she well deserved.

Who Done It Really?

She was so loved by American celebrities that one even announced that he invented it. Performer George Jessel claimed in his 1975 memoir, *The World I Lived In*, that in 1927 he invented the Bloody Mary in

Palm Beach, Florida. Never mind that Jessel was infamous for his far-flung reminiscences in his two previous memoirs. Never mind that Jessel was close friends with John Martin of GF Heublein, the man who, in 1939, bought out Kunnett's failing vodka company and helped invent the Moscow Mule.

As Petiot commented in an article that appeared in Geoffrey Hellman's "Talk of the Town" column in the 18 July 1964 issue of *The New Yorker*: "I initiated the Bloody Mary of today. George Jessel said he created it, but it was really nothing but vodka and tomato juice when I took it over. I cover the bottom of the shaker with four large dashes of salt, two dashes of black pepper, two dashes of cayenne pepper, and a layer of Worcestershire sauce; I then add a dash of lemon juice and some cracked ice, put in two ounces of vodka and two ounces of thick tomato juice, shake, strain, and pour. We serve a hundred to a hundred and fifty Bloody Marys a day here in the King Cole Room and in the other restaurants and the banquet rooms."

Note that Petiot does not say he took it over from Jessel or that Jessel combined the vodka and tomato juice. His vagueness here has led many people to assume he meant both and to take this utterly inconclusive statement as proof that Jessel created the drink.

So where does Harry's New York Bar play a part in all of this beyond that first moment? The drink was called the Red Mary in the 1940s edition of McElhone's *Harry's ABC*. Also in that edition is the College Inn Tomato Juice Cocktail. Made with tomato juice, Worcestershire sauce, celery salt, lemon juice, and **sherry**. Was it that MacElhone was not able to sell the vodka version to patrons after Petiot left the establishment until after the Second World War? Was the reason he renamed it the Red Mary because the initial name offended his Scottish upbringing or British patrons brought up in polite society? We may never know.

What we do know is that one's of the world's most loved morning pick-me-ups has engendered as much spicy conversation and controversy over its origins and that of its bloodline as its famed crystal-clear cousin, the Martini.

But that, friends, is another story.

Negroni

THE KING OF THE APERITIVO

BY DOMENICO CONSTANZO

Good evening, I'll have a Negroni please"
This drink order is heard more than any other during the hours of the *aperitivo* in bars all over Italy. It is a fact that it is one of the Italian's favourite pre-dinner cocktails.

When someone mentions "*aperitivo*" they are talking about that time of the day when friends or colleagues meet for an apéritif simply to sip something good, to enjoy each other's company, and to chat about their day or the upcoming night out on the town.

But where does the word come from? Since ancient times, some Italian communities preceded dinner with an aromatic concoction, either alcoholic or not, to sharpen their appetites. Indeed, the word "*apertitivo*" comes from the Latin term "*aperire*" [opening], which in this case indicates the stimulation of one's hunger! But always, even back then, this was a time to meet and socialize while sipping on something flavourful.

The Negroni in Italy is an authentic institution, for more than 80 years it has been the apéritif *par excellence*. It is ruby colored, with a smell of sweet spices, strong and bitter herbs with juniper berries, orange, and vanilla. Its taste is unmistakable, full bodied and dry. It leaves a balanced pleasurably bitter aftertaste. Due to these peculiarities one could clearly state that the Negroni is the perfect interpretation of an authentic apéritif.

Let's take a step back in time: Florence, in the beginning of the 1920s, with numerous cafés visited by artists, Russian refugees who had escaped from Siberia, foreigners touring Europe, anarchists, and local nobles. Count Camillo Negroni, a Florentine noble who often visited the cafés, involuntarily created what was to become a mixed drink icon.

Count Negroni was passionate about adventure. Having travelled around half the world, he returned to Florence where his experiences and stories brought a great amount of foreign influence to the bars he visited. One of these was Caffè Casoni. Negroni often stopped there to have his favourite apéritif, the Milano-Torino. It was a very popular combination of equal measures of red vermouth and Campari Bitter served with ice and a lemon peel.

Milano-Torino vs Torino-Milano

I deviate slightly to specify that this version of the drink, in reality, is the one that was in vogue in the cafés in Milan. However, when the first version of the Milano-Torino appeared, it was not actually created in Milan but in Turin. In fact, in Turin people also drank the Torino-Milano originally made with equal measures of Amaro Cora and Campari Bitter, according to Camillo Bosco, who is past-president of the Italian Bartenders Association and a historian of Turin's bars and bartenders. When the drink arrived in Milan, the Amaro Cora was quickly replaced with Martini Rosso because the bitter taste of the Amaro Cora wasn't favoured by the Milanese.

From Milano-Torino to Americano

So with the addition of soda, the Milano-Torino soon became the Americano. The origin of the name is still not totally clear, but the most likely hypothesis is that the drink was called the Americano because it contained ice and soda: two very popular ingredients requested by American tourists when they visited Italy.

The Americano
Becomes the Negroni

On an undetermined day between the end of the 1910s and the beginning of the 1920s, Count Negroni walked into the Caffè Casoni and asked the barman Fosco Scarselli to make his Americano with a dose of gin and without the soda to make it stronger and a touch more bitter, while introducing a pleasant juniper aroma to the drink. (Juniper is a very common plant in Tuscany, where Florence is located.)

For the garnish he asked for the lemon peel to be replaced with a half slice of orange, so that everybody would recognise that this wasn't the usual Americano but rather "The Americano" created by Count Negroni. From that day forward, when the Count visited Caffè Casoni, he ordered his usual, arousing people's curiosity. Other patrons began asking for an "Americano like Count Negroni's". Soon this apéritif spread to other cafés in the city.

Because the drink was so successful, Count Negroni asked Fosco Scarselli to name his custom apéritif. With no hesitation he replied, "I would call it Negroni, dedicated to you sir Count, who was the first to drink it".

And that is how the Negroni was born.

Caffè Casoni still serves the original Negroni, even though the establishment's name and management changed, in 1933, becoming the Caffè Giacosa.

The Negroni was entered, in 1961, into the first edition of the official International Bartenders' Association [IBA] recipe book as follows:

1/3 Dry Gin
1/3 Vermouth Rosso (sweet)
1/3 Bitter Campari
Half orange slice garnish
Build into an ice-filled rocks glass

The recipe changed, in 1986, when the IBA instituted the new 10ths measuring system to:

4/10 Gin
3/10 Vermouth Rosso (sweet)
3/10 Bitter Campari
Lemon peel garnish
Build into an iced filled highball glass

But in did not last. By 1993, the recipe returned to its origins, adding a note that in some countries it's typical to serve it with some soda water. Then in 2004, the recipe was published in centilitres and the soda option was deleted.

3 cl Gin

3 cl Vermouth Rosso (sweet)
3 cl Bitter Campari
Half orange slice garnish
Build into an ice-filled rocks glass

The Negoni Becomes Sbagliato

Around 1972 or 1973, the bartender at the historic Bar Basso in Milan, Mirko Stocchetto, accidently poured Brut rather than gin into a Negroni. Being aware of his mistake, Stocchetto offered to remake the drink. But the customer thought as it was a rather hot day the Negroni with sparkling wine would better quench his thirst.

The Negroni Sbagliato [Mistaken Negroni] quickly became very popular at the Bar Basso: It was its signature drink for many years. In fact, by the 1990s, its popularity had spread not only throughout Milan, but all over the country. Nowadays, people simply order a Sbagliato without adding the word Negroni.

Additional variations have joined the Negroni and the Sbagliato. Make it with vodka instead of gin and it becomes a Negrosky. Replacing red vermouth with dry white vermouth makes it a Cardinale. Use tequila in place of gin and you have a Tegroni. Replace the vermouth in a Negrosky with Punt e Mes and you have a Katiusha.

Original, Sbagliato, Negrosky, or Katiusha, the Negroni continues to be the Italians' most beloved apéritif even if its fame has spanned around the world. Not only customers appreciate it, the bartending community does as well, especially in the UK where bartenders have discovered Vermouth Carpano Antica Formula: a product that makes the Negroni even more refined.

However, my advice is to try a Negroni made with Barolo Chinato (a Barolo wine infused with quinine, herbs, and spices that as invented in the 1800s in Serralunga d'Alba) instead of vermouth. In my opinion it's the perfect Negroni: the most noble and the best apéritif to stimulate the appetite.

Inspired Spirits

The Path of the Bartender

BY GARY REGAN

I **was brought up** in the pub business in England. My parents were running a pub when I was born, in fact. The Horse and Jockey, Well i'th' Lane, Castleton, Lancashire. Think working class. Think cotton mills. Think coal mines. Think salt-of-the-earth. It's close to Manchester. When I was two years old, though, Vi, my Mother, convinced Bernard, my Dad, that they should get out of the pub business. A pub isn't the right sort of place to raise such a pretty little innocent lad as our Gary, she told him. Well, something like that. We moved about fifty miles to the Cleveleys end of a town called Thornton-Cleveleys, a seaside resort to which lots of folk new to the almost-middle-classes aspire. Some of those who make it open shops, some run boarding houses—bed & breakfast-type places that sometimes offer lunch and/or dinner, too—and some folk from the industrial north actually manage to retire there so they can spend their last years by the Irish Sea. Vi and Bernard opened a dress shop, about half a mile away from the seafront, and Vi ran that business while Bernard worked at quite a few jobs that he hated until, when I was 12 years old, he managed to persuade Vi that it was safe to get back into the pub business now that I was almost grown. How he pulled it off I'll never know.

The joke, of course, is that I was at one of the most impressionable ages of my entire existence and Dad immediately started to teach me how to clean the beer lines and scrub the floors of the beer cellar with bleach. He showed me how to tap barrels, how to tilt them so you got every last drop out of each one, and he taught me that, if a cask-conditioned beer was cloudy, as a last resort you could add just a tiny amount of British lemonade— lemon-lime soda in the USA—and it would clear up within an hour or so. Bernard was getting me used to the beautiful stench of beer. The Prince Rupert, a smallish, free-standing, modern-at-the-time building with a fair-sized car park, was on a council estate—Americans call them projects—in one of the roughest areas of Bolton, another industrial town close to Manchester. And Bolton's a pretty rough town as it is.

By the time I was fourteen I was tending bar and sneaking beer. Pub life was most definitely for me. Bernard hired a drummer and a piano player—would you believe they called themselves Styx and Tones?—and he also got an emcee who went by the name of Jacko Diamonds. Every Wednesday, Friday, and Saturday nights this trio put on a show and there was a huge knees-up in the pub. Everyone on the council estate did his or her party piece for everyone else on the council estate, and some of them went to great trouble to hone their acts. One guy, for instance, did an Al Jolson routine, complete with blackface, and he was pretty good, too. It wouldn't be politically correct to do these days, but back in the mid-sixties nobody thought anything about that sort of thing. Various other locals performed pop songs, C & W [country & western] numbers, nostalgic ditties from both the world wars—"eeh, them were the good old days, weren't they?"—and various Rat-Pack-style songs. "My Way" was a particular favourite. Too bad nobody nailed that one till Sid Vicious came along. The younger end of the crowd sang pop songs. Beatles, Searchers, Cat Stevens, that sort of stuff. No R&B. No Stones or Yardbirds. Pop songs. Stuff that everyone back then, regardless of age, tended to enjoy.

One guy who showed up from time to time went by the name of Blosh. A tough town needs a town tough. Someone who no one else ever tackles. Nobody in town ever wanted to get on the wrong side of Blosh. Head to toe he measured around five-feet eight-inches. Shoulder to shoulder he was about the same. The man was a cube. His head was shaved bald, and nobody else in a town like Bolton, circa 1966, shaved his head unless they had ringworm or lice. Blosh would appear at the Prince Rupert about twice a year and the room would go silent when he walked in the door. For a minute or so you might hear his name being whispered to one or two people at the far end of the room who hadn't noticed his entrance. They might be laughing at some stupid joke but they soon shut up when they see who walked into the room. People didn't laugh when Blosh was around. He might think they were laughing at him.

Blosh would stroll up to the bar, get himself a pint of bitter—Bernard always served him, and they'd look each other in the eyes and show each other due respect—then Blosh would make his way over to Jacko Diamonds and whisper in his ear. Two minutes later Jacko was telling the room that Blosh was going to sing for us. Blosh made his way onto the stage—a platform just big enough to hold a drum kit, a small upright piano, and one singer. It was raised about eight inches from the floor. Blosh took the microphone, Sammy Ashworth started tickling the ivories, Jimmy the drummer—can't for the life of me remember his last name—picked up a slow beat. All eyes were on Blosh. In a powerful tenor voice that filled the whole fuckin' room with glory, Blosh would belt out one of the most soul-wrenching renditions of Danny Boy you've ever heard. He started out soft. Real soft.

> "Oh Danny boy, the pipes, the pipes are calling
> From glen to glen, and down the mountain side
> The summer's gone, and all the flowers are dying
> 'tis you, 'tis you must go and I must bide."

He fair bellowed the next verse. His voice reached the far corners of the fuckin' universe. I swear it.

> "But come you back when summer's in the meadow
> Or when the valley's hushed and white with snow

'tis I'll be there in sunshine or in shadow
Oh Danny boy, oh Danny boy, I love you so."

Back he came for the next verse. Way down low again.

"And if you come, when all the flowers are dying
And I am dead, as dead I well may be
You'll come and find the place where I am lying
And kneel and say an 'Ave' there for me."

Just a little bit louder now . . .

"And I shall hear, tho' soft you tread above me
And all my dreams will warm and sweeter be
If you'll not fail to tell me that you love me
I'll simply sleep in peace until you come to me."

And one last time he repeats that last line. This time he sings it way slow—one word at a time—and at the top of his fuckin' voice.

"I'll
simply
sleep
in
peace
until
you
come
to
me."

Blosh lingered long on that last word. Real long.

When the song was over there wasn't a dry eye in the house. Blosh would finish his pint, and he would leave peacefully. He didn't want to fuck up in the only place left in town where he could get some stuff off his chest without actually beating the crap out of someone.

For Bernard, the role of the pub landlord came very easily. He was born to play this part, was Bernard. He loved being the center of attraction, and the man had a heart of gold, too. He truly cared for the customers at the Prince Rupert. And it showed. And the regulars loved him for it. Most nights that Styx and Tones played ended with Bernard on the stage putting all he had into "There's No Business Like Show Business." And if he was in the mood, meaning if he has enough gin or rum in his belly, he would belt out some old war songs or music hall ditties, too. One of his very favourites was "The Spaniard That Blighted My Life", a little-known music-hall number that Bernard loved to sing when he'd had a skin-full.

> If I catch Alphonso Spagoni, the Toreador,
> With one mighty swipe I will dislocate his bally jaw.
> I'll fight this bull-fighter I will,
> And when I catch the bounder
> the blighter I'll kill.
> He shall die, he shall die!
> He shall die
> tiddly-i-ti-ti-ti-ti-ti-ti!
> He shall die, he shall die!

For I'll raise a bunion on his Spanish onion
If I catch him bending tonight!

Bernard raised hell with this song. The regulars whooped and laughed and shouted and screamed and laughed some more. He was a regular superstar on the Great Lever council estate was Bernard. He had a voice, too. Not a voice that could have made a living on its own, but he was easy on the ears all the same. Vi just stood back and watched all this go down. She'd shake her head and smile and say, "Oh, Bernard." Words I heard pretty frequently in the Prince Rupert days.

Most people on the Great Lever council estate in Bolton were living from one day to the next cash-wise, and some of them would tap Bernard on the shoulder for the loan of a five-pound note every now and again, but money wasn't the only thing that the customers at the Prince Rupert used Bernard for. He was looked on as a sort of father figure. Someone that people would go to whenever they were in a pickle. On more than one occasion the phone rang in the middle of the night, and a local would say something to the effect of, "Bernard, I think our Billy's dead. I just woke up and I don't think he's breathing. What do I do?" Bernard would call the right people, and he'd go round to the house, too, to sit with the wife while it all went down. Vi—and I didn't learn this till many years later—slipped cash to one or two people who really needed it. The daughter of one of the barmaids, it turned out, needed some medical attention not covered by the National Health program, and Vi came up with the cash they needed to sort it out. We were far from being wealthy, but we had a little more cash than the vast majority of people on that estate.

In return, the pub regulars were fiercely loyal to Vi and Bernard. Fiercely loyal. No strangers ever started any trouble in the Prince Rupert, and anyone who tried to take advantage of any member of the Regan family was quickly set straight. You wouldn't want to mess with these guys, either. People with little cash tend to know how to put a point across. The four years we spent in Bolton turned out to be very important to me in later years. Taught me some core values. That sort of stuff. I made some good lifelong friends, too.

I quickly learned to love the pub game. The landlord's son got quite a bit of respect on the street, and I was staying up till all hours of the morning drinking pints of bitter with the big lads. Eventually "The Five Pints of Bitter Boys," a group of guys around four or five years older than yours truly, started to let me hang with them on Friday nights when they went into the center of town to get drunk out of their minds and try to get laid. We walked from pub to pub to pub drinking pints of bitter or Bacardi and Coke when we were a bit flush. Sometimes we ended up at a casino or nightclub, too. We actually saw Lulu singing "Shout" at the Castle Casino one night.

The long arm of the law never did catch me at my underage drinking game, but I had strict instructions on what to do if

I was ever collared. The law in the sixties exonerated whoever served a minor as long as they went to the trouble of asking how old the customer is. If the kid says he's 18, it was legal to serve him. Simple as that.

"If the police ever catch you," Vi told me in real serious tones, "You tell them that the landlord asked how old you were. You don't go getting other people into trouble. Okay?" Vi didn't lay the law down too often, so I had a pretty freewheeling youth, but when she threw stuff like this at me I knew I'd better listen. She'd never ever have laid a hand on me, but disappointing Vi would have been way more painful than a beating.

The Five Pints of Bitter Lads sometimes ended up with women on our nights on the town, but there weren't any eighteen-year-old chicks that would look twice at a fifteen-year-old boy, even if he did dye his hair grey at the sideburns so he could get into pubs. God I was such an asshole. Not a real obnoxious asshole, but an asshole all the same.

My money for these nights out with the lads came from my tending bar and from Vi and Bernard throwing cash at me for cleaning the cellar or the beer pipes, or helping out in the little shop on the side of the pub where we sold chocolates as well as wine and beer. Sometimes women would walk into the shop with a large pitcher and ask for it to be filled with a couple of pints of draft beer for their husband who was just too tired to come the pub tonight.

When I was sixteen going on seventeen Vi and Bernard snagged The Bay Horse. The pub of Bernard's dreams. It's a genuine Olde England pub, complete with beams and horse brasses. The building is over 300 years old and it stands right next to the train station in the Thornton end of Thornton-Cleveleys, about four miles from the sea-front. We moved back to the coast where I picked up old friendships but still managed to stay in touch with some of my pals from Bolton. We didn't leave the council estate without Bernard throwing one last big-time bash for the regulars at the Prince Rupert, though.

Everyone who ever set foot in the pub over that last four years was there on Vi and Bernard's last night at the Rupert. Pint after pint after pint crossed the bar, and it took half a dozen of us behind the bar to keep the glasses full. We tried not to break anything. Bernard posted a notice over the sink: "Due to the rising prices of bandages, would members of staff please try not to cut themselves while breaking glasses."

Closing time came at eleven in the PM, Bernard locked the front door, and the party carried on. And on. And on. At about two o'clock in the morning the police arrived. The policed liked Bernard and Vi. They got free beer at the Prince Rupert if they tapped on the window after hours. This time, though, it was official business. "You've got to keep the noise down, Bernard. We're getting complaints." The music stopped, Bernard told everyone to keep their voices down, and the cops joined us. "Just one pint, then. We've got to get back to the station."

Two hours later Bernard had to call the police station. "I think you'd better send another car to the Prince Rupert." The cops were way too drunk to drive.

Bernard and Vi taught me much during these pub years, both at the Prince Rupert, and at the Bay Horse. I didn't realize I was being taught any lessons at the time, but I learned by watching them that the most important aspect of the job of a pub landlord or landlady is that they must truly care about their customers. They must care in a very real sense, too. They have to care on a very personal level. Fact is, you see, that nobody ever goes to a pub or a bar for a drink. Why would they? They can drink at home, right? People go to bars for all sorts of reasons. They go to get laid, they go to meet a business partner, they go for conversation, they go to celebrate, they go to cry on someone's shoulder, but they never, never ever, go to a bar for a drink.

And such is the path that the bartender must walk. It matters not whether the man or woman behind the bar can make a great Mai Tai, and creating new masterpiece cocktails is a drop in the bucket compared to the true job of the bartender. We who choose a life behind bars choose a life of service, and we must always remember one thing: Great bartenders don't go to work to serve cocktails. They go there to serve their guests.

Peter Dorellí

THE SILVER HAIRED STORY-TELLER

BY SUE LECKIE

You can't help but love Peter Dorelli. Ask anyone who has spent even a fraction of time with the man, and they will tell you so. Scrape beneath the surface of the "silver haired story-teller, and you'll find even more reasons to hold him in high regard. From the tough times he, as an avowed life-long pacifist, underwent to escape military service in Italy and remain in the UK, to the love laboured by him on making the American Bar at the Savoy the legend it became, he certainly hasn't had it easy. But the focus of the man is clear for all to see, and it is that dedication that has made him head and shoulders above his counterparts.

Roman-born Dorelli didn't set out to become a bartender, that wasn't his passion. In fact, it was his dislike of the future ahead of him rather than any burning desire for something else that was to set him on the (rather winding) path that would eventually see him become one of the world's best known and respected bartenders of modern times. "I'm from a banking family", he explains. "My elder brother was seen as a free man, having clear direction, my younger brother an artist. I had no sign of going one way or the other." So with no clear goal, it was a letter from the army, calling him to service that made him spring into action. And so, "armed with nothing more than a suitcase and a resident handyman permit" he headed to the UK.

Moving across Europe was not that simple in those times. Permits had to be gained, and their terms stuck to, unless changes were made in agreement with the labour exchange. Dorelli, resigned about his situation, set about working his away around the country doing a myriad of domestic jobs: from washing dishes in Cornwall to working as a boiler man in Sloane Square.

After one-and-a-half-years, by his own admission, he became a 'fugitive'. "I couldn't go on doing those jobs, but if I stayed in London, it was hard to get work without having to change my permit. I began taking jobs in bars, pubs and hotels". And suddenly, it would seem, Dorelli had identified his calling in life: "I loved the relationship between the bartender and the customer. I could finally use my personality."

But it was not easy. "I was always watching my back", he resignedly says. "I knew when my moment was over, when I was caught, I'd have to move on". Knowing that being discovered would mean a forced return to Italy , he bit the bullet and went back to working in the domestic market. And it was here that the real the Dorelli story began.

Working for a Jewish couple, he set about once again the tasks of cooking, cleaning and, additionally, hosting cocktail parties. "The man of the house took me aside one day, and declared: 'Why are you here? You can't be doing this forever!' I explained the situation to him, and the next thing I know I am being frog-marched to the labour exchange." The predicament he found himself in was heart stopping. "There are two stamps they use in the office—one to send you home, and one to cancel your permit—essentially giving you freedom to do anything," he excitedly explained. "My heart stopped as the clerk picked one up. My employer, he leaned over and gave me the authority I needed to be taken seriously. The next thing you know, I'm free! I will never forget what he did for me," he says humbly.

Suddenly Dorelli was a free man, with the world at his feet. After "getting drunk for two weeks", he explored several opportunities and avenues in the hospitality industry, which soon led him to believe that he needed something where he could interact with the customer, where a relationship could develop and blossom.

After a few false starts, he headed to the Savoy Group in 1963. "It was the natural choice for anyone who wanted to work behind a bar, but there were simply no vacancies". Instead he was directed to the hotel's sister venue, Stones Chop House. Spread over two floors, the upper restaurant didn't have a bar when he started, but this was soon changed. Dorelli, under the watchful eye of manager, Charles Galiano, coupled with his brother soon made the space, namely the Pebble Bar, their own. Soon he was to head to the Savoy , working for "the mighty Joe Gilmore", but a year later he was back to his beloved Chop House.

The tiny place tucked away near Wardour Street, marked for Dorelli, "the best experience of my life." A surprising declaration perhaps for someone who's name has become synonymous with the Savoy Hotel itself. It fast became the hangout of the movers and shakers of the day—from Roger Moore and Peter O'Toole to Lawrence Olivier and Richard Burton. The reason why? "I was not a bartender. I was a friend," declares Dorelli proudly. A trait that has unquestionably followed him throughout his career. "They felt free. They knew I wouldn't let anyone bother them when they were with us."

On paper, this may look very fortunate, but it is the skill, the passion and the character of the man that got Dorelli to this place, although his humility prevents him from openly admitting this. Instead, he prefers to remain more matter-of-fact about the situation. "In those days, people used to pay to work at the Savoy and its associated venue. But I was fortunate. They gave me the chance to become the official cocktail maker of the company."

Dorelli's term officially began at the Savoy Hotel in 1980, where he and Victor Gower, who had spent 42 years at the hotel, wrangled for power. "He was very much in charge," admits Dorelli. "He expected to have the job single-handedly, so I took on the front of house to avoid clashes". Four years later, the move paid off, as Gower left the company and Dorelli took on the role of Head Bartender formally.

And this is where Dorelli could finally step up to the mark and flex his managerial muscles. A strong work ethic undoubtedly got him the respect he deserved and also assisted in building a fiercely loyal team. "I changed everything, but the most important thing for me was that everyone, no matter of what their position, should be expected to do the same. And in that I included myself. I wanted to train everyone, whether they were bartenders or waiters. I kept nothing back."

Some of the changes to the system were relatively simple. A points system, whereby the higher up the ladder the member of staff was, the higher the percentage of tips they received, incentivised staff. "I also made sure that I kept some money aside each month, and every so often we'd all go out together." The mentality of Dorelli as a manager was simple—they were all in it together, a family.

The approach certainly paid off. "Nobody left the American Bar unless I asked them to," declares Dorelli. And ask he sometimes did. "No matter how good the person or the place, there is only so long they should be there for. Once they had learnt everything they could from me and the American Bar, it was time for them to move on. I always found them somewhere appropriate to take their next steps, but it was crucial for them to move on if they were to progress."

Other changes at the American Bar were more radical. Dorelli broke with tradition and hired female waitresses for the first time in the history of the venue. He put together a team of actresses "who looked a million dollars" and radically changed the nature of the venue. The emphasis was put on the girls being classy: wearing long velvet skirts, fitted blouses ruffled with lace plus a matching choker and velvet cuffs, they instantly pushed takings—and tips—through the roof.

Another move that was to shape the atmosphere of the bar was the hiring of Mike McKenzie, the former pianist at the Dorchester. The chemistry between he and Dorelli was electric; with the bartender frequently causing a stir by sending over trays of drinks to the musician, and a skit ensuing, much to the delight of the guests.

"I did it my way. The only thing I couldn't change was the dress code. That's the only place I failed."

But there were also things that Dorelli simply wouldn't do that made just as much of an impact. "I would never shout on duty. I find that dreadful. You destroy the moment and the magic of that place." No Gordon Ramsay tendencies from our humble Italian.

Most importantly, he never forgot who ruled the roost. "The customer is king," he proudly declares. "You must never, ever lose sight of that. Without making the customer happy, you are nothing." This is perfectly exemplified when you quiz him on his most memorable moments in the bar. With the celebrity crowd at his feet—Dorelli can proudly list those he has served in his time, from the royals to the brat pack as readily as if he were reciting the alphabet—it might be shocking to some that it is the simpler things he relishes from his career. "What used to make my evening? When someone tells me it is their thirtieth anniversary. I want to say to them, thank you for choosing me to celebrate it with." And it is that honesty of soul that makes him so beloved, amongst the industry and his past customers today.

Along with the determination to ensure that the guest was always put first, it was the constant evolution of the venue that Dorelli credits in ensuring its long-term fashionability. "The American Bar always changed. I always believe the bar has to be alive. You should stop and listen. You should be able to hear the heartbeat." Does this still exist today? In a few places maybe, but these are few and far between. Reverting back to the service standards held in such high regard in the past may well be the perfect way of safeguarding the future.

But it is the role and respect of the bartender that Dorelli really holds dear. "For years I have tried to have the position of bartender recognized as that of skilled labour, but I always failed," he claims, (although many would credit him with doing just that, both at his work at the Savoy and additionally during his reign as President of the UKBG [United Kingdom Bartenders' Guild]). "But God bless the mixologist. Now, because of that label, we can say it is a recognized, acceptable profession". He continues: "I'm very grateful that there is now the liquid chef, the liquid king. It's certainly progress."

That progress, however, comes at a price. "We have the celebrity bartender, but where do we go from there?" "What is missing today is time—to the employees. The one thing that holds it together is the hotel bar. It's not so intensive. It is the hotel bar that has the time." So should we revert back to the ways of the formal hotel bar? "I don't say that all about the past was good," admits Dorelli. But the one thing that was good was recognizing that you need time to develop. I see passion, I see interest. I see both of those thing in the younger generation of bartender, but then I also see misuse, and that saddens me considerably. "There's so much talent—not just in London but throughout the country—but integrity has to be maintained. The trust between bartender and customer has to be there."

The problem, says Dorelli, is that bartenders today move through the ranks far too quickly. They simply don't have the basic foundations to build themselves fully. "If I had my day again, I would love to be an ambassador". (Cue a smirk from Dorelli, and frantic dialling from all of the drinks brands!) But his sentiment is serious. "Bartenders can become ambassadors and consultants five or six years after they start in the trade," he dryly states. "What the hell! Where is the foundation? Yes, they may be knowledgeable but can you use it in reality? They bluff their way through simply because they don't have any substance."

And what of cocktails? Surely the man who is arguably the world's most famous bartender must have huge opinions on the past, present and future of the drinks themselves? His response may come as a surprise to the younger generation of mixologists: "It's simple. Any drink you serve should offer value to the customer. It is the overall experience."

There is also a note of caution from the great man. "Make sure you understand the drug you serve too. This is very important. Alcohol is dangerous and you must remember this, otherwise we are going to lose the lot. We need to safeguard our tools and our profession and the authorities are only too keen to limit our freedom."

It is the customers who give Dorelli the spring in his step. The one thing that shows whenever Dorelli talks is a genuine happiness for making a mark on people's lives. "We made something today. Somebody remembers us. We created magic. That is energy; that is our world. We touched their soul." But there are other things. "Without question, the passion I got for drinks comes from Joe Gilmore. He still has that sparkle in his eyes. That's what it is all about", he says passionately. And as for the place that he is always to be associated with? "There's the Dorchester, the Ritz, the Lanesborough, but you can never beat the magic of the Savoy."

The story did end, in 2003. "One morning I woke up and said I don't want to go to work. For me, that's it. Life is too short." and for him, that period of history is closed. "There's more to me than the Savoy. That has finished, but I'm not!" Do not expect to see him land a consultancy gig in preparation for the reopening of the bar anytime soon, but do not expect to see him fade into retirement either.

Dorelli continues to be a role model and a true inspiration. From humble beginnings and a less than ideal start, his story demonstrates that bartenders can have it all. With long-time wife (the magnificent Kay) and a strong family that continues to grow, beside him every step of the way, he demonstrates that late nights don't have to hinder a stable work/life balance. With a raft of other interests to keep him occupied and healthy—chi gong, yoga, and golf to name but a few of his pursuits—a bartender in his twenties would be hard pushed to outdo him on the fitness stakes.

And the work life keeps flourishing, long after the so-called retirement too, (although Dorelli is more conscious than ever to stick with jobs that he genuinely enjoys, and to pick and choose from the raft of appeals he gets from drinks companies to be the face of their brands). From the cocktail demonstrations he continues to do around the world with his long-term pal, Salvatore Calabrese, to his role as Educational Director of the UKBG, where he can indulge his passion for improving standards across the industry and passing on his skills directly to today's up-and-coming bartenders, he is as influential today as he ever was. He's also a regular face on the bar circuit, where he likes to keep an eye on what trends are popular and which mixologists are stealing the show. In fact, I would suggest that it is Dorelli's post-Savoy activities that have really endeared him to the masses and have, in turn, brought him a great deal more satisfaction. Unquestionably, it was his long serving term behind the stick at the American Bar that put his name in lights, but there is a lot more to the man than just that. His career did not finish on his last night there in 2003, in fact, that is when it really started: where we get to see what makes the man really tick, where he gets to be who he really is.

One certainty is that Dorelli has and will continue to earn the respect of those around him. The man who had the legendary Dick Bradsell declare "We are in the presence of a god here", has an army of supporters that continues to grow with every individual he meets. Not because of the cocktails he has created, nor because of the vast knowledge he has on spirits from around the world—although clearly he has both in barrow loads—but because of his commitment to good service, his war cry that the customer is king, and the simple fact that he seeks to carry on learning.

Míguel Boadas

THE DIGNIFIED BARTENDER & HIS DAUGHTER

BY ALBERT MONTSERRAT

Miquel Boadas was undoubtedly the top of the art at preparing everlasting cocktails. He was an outstanding and gifted man, a master of this difficult skill: a born artist, whose work launched the Boadas "school of art" and set a lasting trend.

The conditions around him were always favourable, especially during his tender childhood years: Boadas was born a barman. There were propitious circumstances that led to the development of a personal and a professional personality that would always characterize this *cantinero* [Cuban barman] with his own shining light in the vast cocktail world.

Miquel Boadas Parera was born on a bright morning in La Habana, Cuba, on the 24th of October 1895. He was the first child of Miquel Boadas Guinart and Josefa Parera Marti, Catalan immigrants who had come from the beautiful town of Lloret de Mar on the Mediterranean Costa Brava.

Miquel first saw light in a tavern owned by his parents in La Habana, which was also their home. A bright boy with an agile mind, Miguel helped his father behind the bar. He quickly became an expert with cocktails and drinks as well as with the special features of the business. By the time he was a young man, the bar concealed no secrets from him.

He visited his parents hometown in Lloret de Mar for a long stay, continuing to hone his skills. When he returned to La Habana, his father realised he was destined to became a barman and sent the nineteen-year-old Boadas to work for his cousins, the Sala family, who owned the world famous bar and restaurant La Florida (now known as El Floridita).

Living in a truly cosmopolitan city and constantly serving famous personalities, there was no doubt that Boadas was destined to work in this type of environment no matter where he lived.

Both Miguel Boadas and Constantino Ribalaigua Vert have their names forever linked to Habana's El Floridita, the birthplace of countless famous cocktails—many of them as a result of their inspiration and creative skills. Constantino Ribalaigua eventually acquired the establishment from Boadas' relatives when they decided to retire from their business and return to Madrid, Spain.

During those days, it was not a surprise to see Boadas serving the presidential box at Havana's Jai Alai fronton whenever the occasion required. He fondly remembered the first time he had to serve Cuba's third president Mario García Menocal, who held the office from 1913 to 1921.

Boadas decided to return to Spain, in 1926, and establish his residence in Barcelona. Upon arrival, he paid another visit to Lloret de Mar. There he met his future bride, Maria Ribas Utse, whom he married a year later on 10 May 1927.

In Barcelona, the Maison Dorée, Moka, Nuria, Canaletas, and also a popular beverage stand that was close to the Canaletas Fountain on Las Ramblas near Taller Street were the places where Boadas plied his craft and gained a reputation.

If 1927 was an important year in his personal life, 1933 marked a milestone in his career. In August of that year he achieved a long-cherished desire: He opened his own cocktail bar, one of the first in Spain.

A champion for the profession and the popularization of cocktails in Spain, Boadas expressed his feelings about the dignity of the bartending profession in the press, on radio, and later on television. Another dream came true when he founded, in 1962, the Club Barman (Spanish Association of Bartenders), which he chaired until his death.

The Club Barman came to establish strong ties of friendship amongst the growing number of Spanish bartenders, allowing them to work together for the advancement of professional dignity and the popularization of cocktails. The association conducted cultural and fund-raising events to increase public awareness of the art of responsible drinking.

A whole life linked to the cocktail certifies that Miguel Boadas, the pioneer of the cocktail in Spain, should be called Spanish Barman King. His name continues to thrive in the memories of those who had the joy of knowing him and having him as a friend.

There are pubs and bars, that without knowing why, become associated with certain cities and end up iconic: The Boadas Cocktail Bar symbolizes Barcelona.

On the second of May 1967, Boadas breathed his last and passed away, surrounded by his wife, daughter Maria Dolores, and her husband José Luis "Josep" Maruenda.

In an interview conducted before his death, Miguel Boadas proclaimed:

"My daughter, Maria Dolores, it was my hope that she became the first female bartender. Today, I do not think it is father's pride; I can assure she is. Regarding Josep, my son-in-law, he has assimilated so well what I tried to teach him that he is nowadays a real bartender as well. You may think that good use has been made of my legacy".

The best compliment we can pay Maria Dolores Boadas is that she is an accurate and clear reflection of her father. Born after her father opened Boadas, she was born into the business. Just as it was for her father, everything she was surrounded by in childhood pointed her to her professional direction. When she was nine years old, a very bright Maria Dolores asked if she could help at the bar. Don Miguel thought that this childish wish would be fleeting. But in the course of time her interest increased as that the world of hustle and bustle perfumed by the fragrances of the exotic drinks fascinated her. Don Miguel was amazed and smiled proudly at the clear reality of a fulfilled desire, with the absolute confidence that the legacy of his work was guaranteed.

Maria Dolores stood side by side with her father in her beloved Boadas Bar for more than thirty years, perfecting this blend of art and science. In that time, Don Miguel passed on the best of what he had learnt from both El Flordita in Habana and from his own establishment off Las Ramblas. Thanks to Maria Dolores, The Boadas Bar remains the "Temple of the Cocktail" in Barcelona with its list that includes cocktails dedicated to some of its most famous customers: Joan Miró, Sofia Loren, Cartier.

I cannot stop recognizing in Maria Dolores a very feminine woman who, if you'll forgive the repetition, is the embodiment of professionalism and passion that are absolute.

The Profession

The Secrets of a Bar Charmer

BY PHIL DUFF

"An efficient bartender's first aim should be to please his customers, paying particular attention to meet the individual wishes of those whose tastes and desires he has already watched and ascertained; and, with those whose peculiarities he has had no opportunity of learning, he should politely inquire how they wish their beverages served, and use his best judgment in endeavouring to fulfill their desires to their entire satisfaction. In this way he will not fail to acquire popularity and success."

—Jerry Thomas, 1862

Personal charm is the last great taboo of modern bartending. We can all admit to not having read Tom Bullock, to not possessing a bottle of pine liqueur or an antique cobbler shaker, to never having made the pilgrimage to New York's Milk & Honey. But who wants to admit to not being charming—or not as charming as they could be? In our people-centred industry, it is like saying you enjoy trampling puppies in hob-nailed boots, only not as socially acceptable. I believe this stems from the belief that charm is some mystical ability that is not, and cannot, be learned, and that only greasy, slimy second-hand-car-dealers, sad lonely men who read Neil Strauss' 2005 book *The Game: Undercover in the Secret Society of Pick-up Artists* and scary freaks like Tony Robbins and Derren Brown approach it in any way other than instinctively.

This, of course, is nonsense. You might be lucky to grow up in a household where establishing and maintaining rapport is automatic—large families that eat together at the same time at a single table tend to encourage these skills, hence so many truly charming hospitality professionals are Mediterranean types (Italians, French, Spanish, etc.) But it is totally learnable. It is no different to learning a language, or going to the gym, much more enjoyable and a million times more useful.

Nothing happens in this world—nothing at all—without rapport. And rapport as a learnable skill is becoming mainstream; the highest-rated new TV show in America as we go to press is *The Mentalist* where the main character uses targeted rapport—charm—to solve his cases. Famously, Band Aid & Live Aid, the global charity song and concert that was held in 1985, raised £180 million. Three years later, during a lunch with then-French premier Mitterrand, Live Aid organizer Bob Geldof extracted a commitment to an extra 180 million in aid. Over lunch! Have things changed since?

> REPORTER: *"You move in the highest circles [Bill Gates, Warren Buffett, the G8, world leaders]. Do you think*

that the important decisions that affect us all are taken behind closed doors?"

BONO: *"It was quite shocking to discover how important personal chemistry was. Unexpected cooperations would occur because people realized they could laugh with each other. That made a deep impression."*

—From an interview with *Nieuwe Revu*, Amsterdam, February 2009

I have made a study of the elements of charm in the last few years, and it does get a little scary at times. It is so powerful. Appearance, for instance, is a component of charm. Do you know what the strongest correlation is for becoming president of the USA? It isn't particular policies, or voting records, or political affiliations, or which party or business success. It is height. The tallest guy tends to win. Seventeen presidents since 1896 have been taller than their opponents, while only eight have been shorter—a 68 percent victory for the beanpoles. That percentage rose when TV became widespread in the late 1950s and appearance became even more important. The tall guys won 10 out of 14 elections from Eisenhower in '56 up to and including Barack Obama in 2008. That's a 71 percent success rate. Wow.

It holds true in the world of business, too: 58 percent of Fortune 500 CEOs are six feet tall or taller. But only 14 percent of American males are six feet tall or above. You don't get the corner office just by being tall, but if it's between you and a sub-six footer, start ordering the new carpet.

For those of you—like me—closer to Mini-Me and Shrek than Shaquille O'Neal and George Clooney, there is hope: studies have proven that exogenous beauty (hair style, clothes, makeup) is just as important in being seen as beautiful as endogenous attributes such as height, hair length, physique and having symmetrical facial features.

Charm, **rapport**, persuasion, or (if you are of a paranoid turn of mind) manipulation is the fundament of management skills, and management is the most highly-paid job in the world. In the context of a bar, being able to get other people—colleagues, guests, even your owner or manager—to "buy in" to your ideas, means you can, unless your ideas are distilled horse crap, make everyone happy. A great experience for your guests, fun work and more tips for you and your colleagues and higher sales and profits for the manager/owner.

In studying charm, I often feel as if I was wearing blinkers my whole life, and I hope I can help you remove yours. It will not be hard—I mean, an attractive, well-dressed, successful person like yourself should have no trouble with this.

The Self-Serving Bias

You, me, all of us, are subservient to what is called the self-serving bias. We see ourselves in a positive light and others in a less positive light. When we make a right decision it is because we are attractive, intelligent, successful people. When we make a wrong decision, it was the other guy's fault, it was the wrong question, there's a global financial crisis and by the way, the dog ate my homework. For a hilarious explanation of the self-serving bias, rent or download *One Night At McCool's*. At one stage, using separate flashbacks, two different characters (played by Matt Dillon and Paul Reiser) are remembering a night at McCool's bar. In each case, they remember themselves as being cooler, sharper, more decisive and in control, while the other is remembered as less proactive, drunker, and more of a loser. This, then is the self-serving bias.

The self-serving bias flourishes because we lack the one thing that only another person can give us: hepatitis. Only joking! I mean perspective, of course. Nobody can see themselves as others see us. We interact with the world through our senses, which our brains then filter and present to us as experiences. The process of filtering allows all our own prejudices, ignorance, errors in judgment and the self-serving bias full rein, so what appears to us as an "experience" may bear no more relation to the reality than a hamburger does to a Chateaubriand. The opposite is also true: we want to communicate X, but by the time our brains have filtered that desire and expressed it verbally, visually or through touch (aroma too, if what you wanted to communicate was "I just ate a curry"), it may emerge as Y. It doesn't matter what you want to communicate, it only matters what you do communicate.

Whenever we ask other people for "their honest opinion" we so very rarely get it. This is because we tend to ask people who are in some way invested in our lives: in the worlds of the Dragon's Den investors, "family, friends and fools". They do not want to hurt our feelings so they soften their words—in effect, they "project" their own self-serving bias. Their words are consequently as much use as a chocolate jockstrap.

Do you have someone in your life who doesn't give a damn about you one way or the other—that is, positively or negatively? That is the person to ask for an honest opinion. No-one else's matters.

Once you have one honest opinion, go get some more. At a certain point, you will have a trustworthy image of yourself. Do not ignore this. If everyone says you are pleasant enough but very annoying when talking about your own area of expertise, you must accept this as gospel and not fall prey to the self-serving devil on your shoulder whispering "but if they only knew how cool Boker's bitters really are they'd love them as much as I do!". You must remember: the goal is to be charming, that is, to make people like you so that they will do what you want. This all sounds very Manchurian Candidate, but it isn't. Because what you want is for people to have a good time with fine drinks and sparkling conversation, right?

What, Then, Is Charm?

would say it is a collection of the following elements:

- Appearing pleasant and attractive.

- Relaxing the other person.

- Building and maintaining rapport using body language, word choice, intonation, pacing and leading.

- Using common sense and choice architecture to deliver guests a great experience.

I'm writing about this for all bars, and writing in quite general terms. Charm is in no way reserved for white-collar bartenders in up-market cocktail lounges. The way in which you are charming doesn't matter, it just has to be appropriate for the situation. One of the most charming bartenders I know is a large, scary-looking man named Zardoc, who is bartender/bouncer at a rock 'n' roll bar in Amsterdam's red-light district. In Hell's Angels bars like his, it is (Zardoc tells me) seen as charming and complimentary to say "Nice tits!" to a young lady possessed of an impressive rack, and, indeed, her gentleman companion will also be charmed by your courteous compliment. Similarly, "appearing pleasant and attractive" requires very different clothes and preparation for a night in Excalibur (where Zardoc works) than it does in The Dorchester—a white-jacketed sleeve-gaitered dandy is as unpleasant and unattractive in Excalibur as would be most of Zardoc's regulars in The Dorchester.

Appearing Pleasant & Attractive

As we have seen, this is important. We humans, hairless apes that we are, evolved and along the way it would appear several traits have become genetically hard-wired. Allen and Barbara Pease's excellent 2004 book *Definitive Book of Body Language* goes into great detail, for instance:

- We are programmed to respond positively to baby faces (chubby cheeks, smile, wide eyes) because neglecting babies wasn't a very good evolutionary strategy, hence we react positively when someone smiles at us, making their cheeks more chubby and their eyes wider.

- We react submissively to tall, healthy, confident, attractive people, recognizing desirable genetic traits that we would like to pass on to our offspring (Although I speak from bitter experience when I say "I'd like to pass on your desirable genetic traits to our offspring" sucks as a pick-up line).

We like looking at attractive people, and while we are looking we listen to what they are saying. Tall attractive people are, in addition to being attractive, authoritative: we listen to them and follow their orders. And if they have a clear speaking voice, we are putty in their hands. In the superb 2008 book *Outliers: The Story of Success*, Malcolm Gladwell details how a good-looking tall man with a deep voice was elected president almost entirely because of his looks. Warren Harding turned out to be just about the worst president ever, but perhaps one of the most presidential-looking.

Eleven Things To Make Yourself More Attractive

1 **Shower and (gentlemen) shave** or trim your beard each day. Trim your fingernails and nose hair every week and tweeze your eyebrows. Use an odourless deodorant daily. Spritz yourself lightly with perfume or aftershave before your shift begins. Ladies: apply makeup sparingly but expertly.

2. Wear clothes that fit. Most women do, most men do not. Wear clothes that are clean and ironed with no rips or holes or other defacements.

3. Wear clothes that look good on you, and that you feel good wearing. The clothes you may want to wear may not look or feel good on you. But if you do not feel good wearing clothes that look good on you, it is time to get with the program, soldier.

4. Wear clean, polished shoes. Wear them once and then polish them again. Ladies—and I say this knowing how painful it can be to wear them—wear heels as high as is practical for you, if you can. (I used to play rugby, and sometimes at rugby-club dinners... .)

5. Wear your hair in a flattering style, wash and condition it daily. And if you style it with gel or some such, always have some at work so you can touch it up during the evening.

6. Wear attractive accessories that complement your clothes: Watch, rings, belt, tie, pocket square, non-dangling jewellery, etc.

7. Take at least one full minute to look at yourself in a full-length mirror before your shift begins. Make changes accordingly.

8. Look healthy. There is no short cut. You must be healthy. Not hung-over, but well rested, well-fed, with health oozing out of your pores. A light sun-tan helps, too.

9. Be confident. Few things are as attractive as confidence. If you do not feel confident, fake it. You will be surprised at how

confidence is self-generating. Much of it will come from being well-dressed in clean clothes that look good on you, well-fed, well-rested, healthy and happy. Simply imagine that you feel happy, secure and confident, and then go get 'em.

10. Smile. Smile when you meet someone, when you say goodbye, and at every opportunity in between. You might feel like a lobotomy patient, but no-one will ever notice that your smile is not always sincere. They will be too busy enjoying your charming company. And, the more you smile the more positive you will feel towards others.

11. Take a course in public speaking. Learn how to project, how to pause in your sentences for effect, how to make jokes effectively, and how to get your point across. Learn to speak impressively and authoritatively—and then learn to listen, because charm is as much about letting others talk as it is about talking to them.

Relaxing

"A gentleman is someone who always puts everyone else at their ease."—Unknown

Going to a bar can be very stressful. A first date, drinks with an important client, meeting friends that might include ex-girlfriends, potential husbands, former business associates and at least one person you wouldn't spit on if he was on fire: Social situations are increasingly complicated. You have to choose what to wear, perhaps make a reservation or choose a time for everyone meet up, and find the place. If it's your first time you don't know what to expect, what the drinks cost, who else will be there. And then when you're inside you may have to leave your date / client / girlfriend behind and fight your way to the bar, then fight for attention from the bartender. If it's tableside service you might be confronted with a menu full of exotic, obscure, and worrying options. What the hell is Batavia arrack? What if I mis-pronounce "Caipirinha"? What if the waitress laughs at me? Or my date? Or the client?

Relaxation is key. If you can, make sure the door to the bar opens inwards (welcoming guests in) instead of outwards (effectively pushing them away before they even enter!). If it is at all possible, try to greet the guest as soon as he or she come in. If you can't have someone greet them and take their coats, then at least make sure they get smiled and waved at by a bartender or waiter. Point them towards a coat rack. Gesture them to an empty table or seats at the bar. Keep smiling. I am often asked what the best way to welcome a guest is. It is to say "Welcome!". Yeah, duh, right? But it is so often forgotten. Follow it up with a thank-you. "Thanks for coming along tonight!". Never mention a guest's previous visit if he is with someone that you do not both know, and even then it is better to wait for him to bring it up himself.

Now for a compliment. Always give a guest a compliment. Compliment ladies on their clothes, shoes, hair, jewellery or handbag. Compliment the gentleman on his clothing, or (if you are sure it is a couple) on the beauty of the lady. Compliment a group on how attractive and fun they look. Do not worry about being "fake". We are all fake, in different settings and with different people. I talk very differently to my mother than I do to a client, or a guest, or a pretty girl in a bar, and so do you. We are inseparable from the masks that we wear. You should find something about everyone to make a sincere compliment upon, and if you cannot, you are not looking hard enough. Don't make a sarcastic joke or undermine your own compliment. Be sincere.

Rapport

You do not need to like someone to have rapport with them: it is just that we tend to unconsciously develop rapport with people that we like, and who like us back. But you can develop rapport with anyone. The single largest component of rapport is observation: consciously observing what people say and do and reacting accordingly. This topic is covered brilliantly in British mentalist Derren Brown's 2004 TV series *Trick of the Mind*. In series two, Brown so effectively uses targeted rapport, word choice, intonation and setting that he manages to convince a well-known actor (Simon Pegg) that his ideal present (which Brown has prepared) is a BMX bike. This despite the fact that, weeks before, Pegg had written down "leather jacket" on a piece of paper, sealed it in an envelope and carried it around in his wallet, where he must have noticed it once a day at least. At the end, Pegg is visibly flabbergasted to discover that he had written down "leather jacket": he really, truly wants nothing more than a BMX bike. That is how powerful rapport can be. (The episode can be viewed on YouTube.)

Body Language

When I read the quote from Jerry Thomas that started this article—and it's the very first "hint" in his *Bar-Tender's Guide*—I cannot but think that JT was writing about reading and reacting to body language. Notice that he at no time mentions making great drinks or even good drinks. No, just satisfying "desires he has already watched and ascertained" in order to "acquire popularity and success." Ol' JT in his heyday was making the equivalent of $220,000 a year in today's money, and I for one would attribute that to his skill in reading guests, not because he steeped his own bitters.

Study after study confirm that total inter-personal communication is 38 percent body language, 45 percent intonation and just 7 percent verbal, i.e. word choice. Most people do not consciously observe or adjust their body language—but I am sure you have at least once, just moments after meeting some-one, made a snap judgment about whether you like him or not? That's body language. You may not even have heard the gentle-man in question speak, but you just do not like him. The chap in question might eventually get into your good graces, but he is going to have to work a lot harder than if you had liked him at first glance.

One aspect of body language is that we see much more than we think we do. Malcolm Gladwell's great 2006 book *Blink: The Power of Thinking Without Thinking* explains "micro expressions", tiny facial expressions that we make for less than a second, that cannot be differentiated by the naked eye, only in slow-motion reply on video. But our eyes do see them when they occur, and we react accordingly—but not consciously. And that's your snap decision, which is very often the correct one (see Gerd Gigeren-zer's 2007 book *Gut Feelings: The Intelligence of the Unconscious* for further reading).

Body Language Precepts

1 **Body language** expresses how you feel, but it also influences how you feel. If a guest is asking for recommendations but is sitting there in a "closed" posture—arms and legs crossed, perhaps the head lowered and tucked in slightly—he isn't really interested in recommenda-tions. He might be tired, cold or maybe intimidated by you, your bar or the drinks list, but for whatever reason, he is "closed". If you hand that guest an open menu, lean forward just a little, and talk just a bit more softly than you normally would, he will open his hands (to grab the menu) and lean forward, which will probably force him to uncross his legs. Instantly, you have created an "open" guest that cannot help but be more receptive to your suggestions. Body language both expresses and influences your feelings.

2. Body language is also language. You can no more draw reliable inferences from one posture of body language than you can by overhearing one word of a conversation. You have to follow someone for a while and establish a "baseline" of their body language in different situations before you can accurately read it. And body language is culture-specific: Scandinavians use much less, and different, body language than do, say, Spaniards. In some cultures, nodding your head means "no" while shaking it means "yes".

3. Body language is contextual. A lady might be crossing her arms and legs, indicating a "closed" state of mind. This may be due to (a) a long day at work, so she needs to relax mindlessly, or (b) the fact that she feels cold or (c) she's wearing a low-cut top and a short skirt. Context is all, and it must dictate your approach.

4. Body language rules. If someone is verbally saying A, but, through body language, communicating B, we will deduce he is

saying B, or at the very least that he is not being honest when he says A. We often pick up on this as a "gut feeling".

Rapport can be quickly established through body language by pacing. This is nothing more than, in a very general way, copying the other person's body language, breathing rhythm, blinking rhythm, word choice and speaking rhythm. Don't copy the other person's moves exactly—that gets creepy quickly—but if the person you're speaking to runs her fingers through her hair, you could scratch your neck, that sort of thing. She smiles, you smile. After a while of this you can start to match the other person's breathing and blinking rhythm. You can even mirror word choice:

> HER: "*...and I was just looking at this guy, like, what did I ever see in him?*" (*she's using visual words*)

> YOU: "*Yeah, I see what you're saying, he must have looked like a fool. Ha ha ha!*" (*...and so are you, you clever thing!*)

Once you have established rapport, you can begin leading. Change your breathing, or make a movement, or change your word choice and see if the other person adjusts to follow you. If you've never done anything like this before, when you start to lead successfully after pacing for a while, it will be your

"Whoa!" moment. You'll have to stifle a "BU-WA-HA-HA-HA!" or two.

Words

The words you use are only 7 percent of communication but they are still important. The right words can awaken powerful memories and the accompanying emotions, all anchored by aroma and flavour memories, like Proust biting into a tea-dunked madelaine in his semi-autobiographical, seven volume novel *A la Recherche du Temps Perdu* [Remembrances of Things Past] (1913-1927). It's no coincidence that the ridiculously successful Harry Potter books contain lots and lots of descriptions of eating and drinking. And are you ready for another "duh! moment? You must listen to what people say. Not drift off, wondering what your nickname would be if you got a job with The A-Team. Not surreptitiously text-messaging. Listen. In the world of sales, it is often said that a customer will tell you how they want you to sell something to them. Here, with thanks to Derren Brown, an excellent example:

> YOU (Bartender): "Welcome sir! Thanks for dropping by. What can I get such a good-looking young man about town like yourself tonight?"

> GUEST: "I was looking for a gin and I saw your back-bar, I see you have a lot......."

YOU: *"Yes, do have any favourites you like to drink?"*

GUEST: *"Well, how about that one there in the pink neon bottle with the flashing lights on it? That looks cool!"*

YOU *(stifling a pained expression)*: *"Well, to be quite honest, that one's a bit, er...crap. It's cold-compounded rubbish made by drunken chimps, ordered on consignment and sold only to gullible fools who watch more than one reality TV show per week. Would you like to try Juniperbomeateray Emerald? It's pot-stilled Bermondsey-style with just a hint of African tree-hound carcass (and you put the bottle in the guest's hands).*

GUEST *(looking as if you just handed him a rotting tree-hound carcass)*: *"Er, no, it's OK, tell you what, I'll have a beer....."*

See what happened? The guest was using words that made it very clear he was only interested in how the gin looked ("I was looking...I saw...I see...That looks..."), while the all-knowing bartender had gotten past the "looks" of bottles years ago to concentrate on their inherent qualities—and failed to really listen to what the guest was saying. In the above situation, a bartender who was better at listening could have just sold the guest the gin in the flashy bottle, or at least a gin that was a good compromise between quality and flashy packaging. Here's how it might have gone:

GUEST: *"Well, how about that one there in the neon bottle with the flashing lights on it? That looks cool!"*

YOU: *"I see, I see, it IS spectacular, isn't it? I must say, you really know your gins. When I'm looking for a gin – like you are – I always look for a good balance of a beautiful package and an absolutely delicious, well-made gin, don't you? How about this G'Jewelarioselleouth Air Force Strength? It's proper distilled gin and look! the bottle glows in the dark!!"*

GUEST: *"Awesome dude! (high-fives you). Make mine a double!"*

Intonation

A whopping **38 percent** of communication, intonation is the speed at which you speak, the emphasis you place on words, and your use of strategic pauses to get and keep the audience's attention. It is one of the first skills that actors learn, and most of us know at least one person, actor or not, who can hold a group spellbound as he tells the most mundane of stories, or the most unfunny of jokes.

The primary exercise is to stand where a friend of yours cannot see you, and try saying a normal word (I favour "elbow") in at least five different ways—for example, aggressively, seductively, whiny, inquisitively and bored. Get your friend to write down each time what emphasis he thinks you are putting on the words, and compare notes afterwards.

Pausing for effect, done correctly, has the audience hanging on your every word. It is used brilliantly by most politicians, who all seem to have the same media trainer. Try speaking this sentence, clearly and confidently with a one-second pause in between each line:

> *"It is very important indeed*
> *To know that distilling, especially double-distilling*
> *Is essential to the integrity of the spirit*
> *And we*
> *Must always demand*
> *That our spirits be double-distilled"*

This, of course, is nonsense. But read with confidence in a clear voice with the correct pauses, it sounds like the freakin' Gettysburg Address.

The speed at which you speak is also important: a precept of establishing rapport—watch the Derren Brown/Simon Pegg video again if you have not yet—is that you can overwhelm the other person into agreement with a rapidly-spoken chain of sentences. Quickly rattling off thoughts, facts, figures (politicians are excellent at this) overwhelms listeners, so much so that when you pause very slightly in your high-speed delivery and ask the other person for a yes or a no, or to do something or not to do, they will do exactly as you ask, if you have already established rapport through relaxation, pacing and leading.

Common Sense
& Choice Architecture

You know what I mean—you do, don't you? Because I know you. You're a Caucasian male, live in a large-ish city, preferred the original *Star Wars* trilogy, use a Mac or a tricked-out Windows PC, own an iPod or similar and have travelled to bar and cocktail conventions in cities like New Orleans, London, Amsterdam, Paris, Berlin or Sydney. I bet as you sit there reading this there's a drink within arm's reach. I'm right, aren't I? It's a comfortable reading light and you're sitting in your favourite spot. You love classic cocktails, hate vodka, dislike flair bartending, disdain disco drinks, use Facebook, love whiskey, use a jigger and I bet you own at least one copy of *Diffordsguide*. And you're a good-looking guy too, well-dressed, popular with the ladies and intelligent. You've read this far, right? Well done!

The above paragraph might sound a bit like mind-reading, but it is just common sense. Most people who buy a specialist book like this one will agree broadly with the statements above. There are more women than men in mixology (sadly), more city dwellers than rural, and of course you're sitting comfortably—duh. This, more then anything, is the common sense of charm. See what everyone sees. Do—or say—what no-one does.

With great power comes great responsibility. It is all well and good to have superhuman powers of persuasion, but in a bar setting, you are employing them to make money. Bars make money by being viable over the mid-to-long term: having consistent sales for a long enough time to pay off any loans and make some real money. If you use your skills to overload a guest with food and drink, you make a lot of money one night and probably very little thereafter—you "burned" them.

The goal is to get your guests to return. If they return, you will always have another chance to sell them something extra. But if they ever get an inkling—and remember, body language, intonation etc. work both ways—that you are milking them , they will not return.

Choice Architecture

It **is possible** to heavily influence the choices that guests make in your bar because you, handsome chap/ gorgeous lady that you are, are a Choice Architect. You choose which options to give to a guest. You design the choosing system, as it were. A few precepts of choice architecture:

- **Humans want instant satisfaction.** They want that new car / perfect wedding / hot date / easy date / Staggerac / double-layer limoncello cheesecake NOW, damnit, and the bill/divorce/hepatitis/hangover/extra ten kilos, well, that's a problem for the future. One Dutch anti-drinking campaign uses this principle in it's ads: they feature the enjoy-ably onomatopoeic tagline: "De Kater Komt Later" [The Hangover Is Later]. It is easy to convince a guest of anything involving in-stant gratification. Staggerac! Because hey, they walked into your bar. It's not like they thought it was a health-food store, now was it?

- **Difficulty.** We do not have to make choices about some things often enough to become expert at choosing, and some things are in-sanely complicated anyway. Most people only get married and buy a house a few times in their lives, for instance. Guests who don't visit nice bars often, or don't drink nice liq-uor in them, are unpractised. And let's be honest, choosing what to drink in a nice bar, even for practised experts, is not easy.

- **Feedback.** It is only by seeing our "mistakes" that we learn. We only learn what drinks, and crucially, which kind of drinks, we like by trial and error. Most bartenders are relatively expert in drinks because they drink more, more often and perhaps with fewer budget constraints, than "normal" people. We typi-cally know far more about food than drinks because this trial-and-error is usually done by our parents when we are young in regard to food. ("Tonight Mom's made curry!") But if your daddy was conducting a vertical Man-hattan tasting with you while you were still wearing shorts to school, it's a wonder you haven't been on Jerry Springer already.

- **Knowing Stuff.** If you have never drunk whiskey, it is no help at all to hear that Greenore Irish whiskey tastes similar to Weller's Kentucky bourbon. When we have to choose unfamiliar products (Jefferson's whiskey?) in unfamiliar settings ("What is a speakeasy anyway? I could barely find the damn place! They should put a sign outside.....") , we evaluate them in terms of what we do know – which is often not helpful. A teenage girl (in countries where teenage girls are legally allowed to drink alcohol) ordering a James Bond Martini has probably never drunk a cocktail before, certainly not one like this, and probably never been in a nice bar like yours. All she DOES know is the name of a cocktail. She needs to be Nudged.

- **More choice does not help**. It frustrates. The libertarian model of decision-making –that we are all super-intelligent, rational and require only many different options from which we can flawlessly select the best one – is flawed. If a guest has never drunk a cocktail before, a 50 drink menu will not help him. A 20-drink menu will not. A 10-drink menu, perhaps, will.

In the *Nudge: Improving Decisions about health, Wealth, and Happiness*, authors Richard H Thaler and Cass R Sunstein introduce the concept of libertarian paternalism. This can be summed up thus:

1. Allowing people to do anything they want (libertarian) but...

2. Designing systems to "nudge" them in a "good" direction (paternalism)

The essential idea behind libertarian paternalism is that people are both stupid and lazy, and let's be honest, at certain times and on certain topics, we all are.

Nudging & You

Wouldn't you like to be able to nudge people to drink better? Maybe even help them discover some of the hidden bargains on your menu? Steer them 'twixt the Scylla of advertising and the Charybdis of peer pressure? Then make it easier for them to order what is better for them—in your expert opinion—and harder to order what is not. Choose something that you would like to have happen—guests ordering faster, drinking better, selling more high-margin liquor, champagne and cocktails instead of low-margin high-volume beer and wine, whatever. Now tweak the systems you have for helping people decide. (If you're following me, this is another BU-WA-HA-HA! moment). Now sit back and observe. Some examples might include:

- If you have interior-lit glass-fronted refrigerators for beer, wine and soft drinks, order blackout sticker for the doors, so guests will not be entranced by the backlit bottles therein. For bonus points, have the stickers paid for by a liquor brand, or with a stencil of a cocktail name cut into it so the light shines through. Have a lighted glass-fronted champagne fridge somewhere at eye level, or perhaps a large champagne bucket full of crushed ice and various bottles of champagne, right in the middle of the bar.

- Remove all mention of everything except for champagne, liquor and cocktails from the menu. Guests can order them—and you have to assume a bar will have them—but you are nudging them towards what you consider to be better. Only include a dozen of the cocktails you'd like to sell, six to eight champagnes, and no more than thirty brands of liquor, tops.

- Have a one-line, twelve-word description for each cocktail, liquor brand and champagne; no more, no less. Include a simile of how it tastes: "lemon-biscuit flavours" describe a good bourbon sour, while a Sazerac contains anise-cherry flavours from the Peychaud's. Help people to choose between unfamiliar options in an unfamiliar setting.

- Remove all the latent POS and branding you have for everything except liquor, cocktails and champagne. Beer signs, pour mats, branded straws, napkins, bartender bottle openers, bar caddies, fridges, everything. Unplug the beer tap lights.

- Put the products you want to sell at eye-level on the back bar, slightly right of centre (studies show 70 percent of guests approaching a bar haven't decided what to order, they scan the back bar and their gaze ends in the middle of the back bar, slightly to the right). If your back bar looks like you sell glassware, sort it out.

- Make sure your offer is strong enough to support your choice architecture. Re-invent your whole drinks list around champagne, cocktails and liquor. You will need both cheaper and more expensive options, familiar as well as obscure brands, drinks that are visually appealing, that appeal to different age groups, etc. Your offer must be good before you start nudging guests towards it, otherwise you, sir, are polishing a turd.

One Final Exercise
& A Creepy Quote

Jim Sullivan and Phil Roberts, authors of the 1995 book *Service That Sells!: The Art of Profitable Hospitality*, pioneered the Sullivan Nod, which is just about the most powerful sales technique there is in a bar. I guarantee when you read what followed you will laugh out loud or at least smile but here's the thing: it works. Like, nine times out of ten. No-one ever notices you're doing it. It's so powerful you have to use it altruistically: you can literally sell anything to anyone, but you must remember the only goal is a satisfied guest who will return—"burning" a guest by overloading him with too much expensive booze on one trip may kill your future possible sales to him.

The Sullivan Nod: Slowly nod two times as you say the name of the brand or drink you'd like the person to choose.

First relax your guest and build rapport. Then, let's imagine your guests asks for a recommendation and says he likes whiskey. If you're recommending a Sazerac alongside a Manhattan or an Old-Fashioned, it would go like this:

"There's the Sazerac (nods twice), The Manhattan or the Old-Fashioned. Which one would you like?"

Lets make it even more powerful. Smile as you nod when you say "Sazerac", but don't smile when you say the other two names. Smiling makes our eyes wider and our cheeks more childlike, and humans are genetically programmed to respond positively and gullibly to child-faces.

"There's the Sazerac (smiles and nods twice), The Manhattan or the Old-Fashioned. Which one would you like? "

And let's take advantage of another nifty phenomenon called Primacy and Recency: we tend to remember what comes first and last, and forget everything in between as "noise". So as well as smiling and nodding, let's repeat Sazerac at the end of the list as well:

"There's the Sazerac (smiles and nods twice), The Manhattan, the Old-Fashioned and the Sazerac (smiles and nods twice), Which one would you like? "

And (stifle your BU-WA-HA-HA! Yes, you there at the back) let's make it utterly bullet-proof by shaking our head when we say Manhattan and Old-Fashioned. Shaking your head is the ultimate "no" and we learn it immediately we're born: It's how a child indicates it has had enough of the milk flowing from a breast or a bottle.

"There's the Sazerac (smiles and nods twice), The Manhattan (shakes head), the Old-Fashioned (shakes head) and the Sazerac (smiles and nods twice), Which one would you like? "

This will put your success rate with this "sale" in the 95 percent to 100 percent range. But only if this was the right drink to recommend. Your offer must be good.

> CYPHER: *You know, I know that this steak doesn't exist.*
> *I know when I put it in my mouth, the Matrix is telling*

my brain that it is juicy and delicious. *After nine years,
do you know what I've realized?*

*(Pausing, he examines the meat skewered on his fork.
He pops it in, eyes rolling up, savouring the tender beef
melting in his mouth.)*

Ignorance is bliss.

AGENT SMITH: *Then we have a deal?*
—from the 1999 motion picture *The Matrix*

The Guild of Remarkable Barmen

THE HISTORY OF THE UKBG

BY LYNN BRYON

1934

In a pre-war Britain, many bartenders worked in elegant hotels and on just as elegant ocean liners. Others worked on the large ferries that travelled between Europe and the United Kingdom.

It was suggested, 1933, that perhaps it would be a good idea to have a forum whereby bartenders could talk to each other about their trade. Communications were not as sophisticated as they are today. Telephones were new instruments, mobile phones were fantasies of the future. A fax machine and the internet were ideas out of science fiction movies.

In this social context, the idea of a guild for bartenders was a great concept, bringing people together to discuss issues, share information, and enjoy the social interaction.

A group of London-based bartenders, including WJ Tarling (Jimmy) from the Café Royal, Harry Craddock from the prestigious Savoy hotel, Billy Whitfield of the Florence Restaurant, the well-known Mr Paul (Bernard Paul), the bar manager of the Grosvenor House hotel on Park Lane put together a cocktail competition at which they discussed setting up a guild.

In August 1934, the thought became a reality. Harry Craddock was elected as the inaugural President of the United Kingdom Bartenders Guild. This was a momentous occasion.

According to the organisation's charter the group's objectives included:

- Assist in training apprentices

- Foster employment

- Provide a proper registration of new cocktails (the Guild does not do that now)

- Provide free legal advice (the Guild does not do that now)

- Publish a magazine titled *The Bartender* (this is now done via the website)

- Act in a manner that is generally beneficial to the trade

The UKBG's aims have remained the same into the 21st century.

The guild then subdivided the United Kingdom into regions: Scotland, Northern, London and South West.

Sadly, there are no records of the first meeting on file in Jim Slavin's Linlithgo office, where he has archived all guild documents dating back to its the second year. "Of the actual birth date [of the UKBG] there are no records at all. The first edition of the archive is missing." Jim Slavin reports.

Every piece of paper has a story or two to narrate.

At that first August meeting it was decided that McDonald Press of Pall Mall would publish *The Bartender*, which was distributed only to members. And it was decided that the twelve monthly issues would be bound into an annual edition. Notes from the first annual general meeting noted that 3000 copies were published in the preceding calendar year.

In those days, there were quite a lot of bartenders coming to and leaving the country. Many more than do now. There literally were bartenders—and consequently members—from all over the world.

The guild established branches in most English-speaking countries that did not already have such a professional association. Australians joined from such glamorous tourist areas such as Coolangatta, the Royal Hayman Hotel on the world-famous Great Barrier Reef, from Melbourne, Sydney, and Townsville.

Bartenders from Austria, France (Biarritz), Belgian Congo, Canada, Ceylon Egypt, French Guinea, Ghana, Holland, and Thailand also joined as overseas members. Air and sea stewards enrolled, too.

But most of the members worked in and around London's top hotels.

The Bartender published theatre reviews and stories of life in the capital city. The first cocktail competition covered in its pages was the British Empire Cocktail Competition, which was held in Grosvenor House from 11-17 September 1935. The first five days were taken up with first-round heats; the last day saw the intense competition for semi-final places and the finals.

The first winner was Bert Nutt of the Grand Hotel in Bristol, with his drink, The Cliftonian, which consisted of Swedish Punch, Grand Marnier, Booth's Gin, and orange juice. No garnish was recorded. They were not quite the thing back then.

Details of the first annual dance, which was held in September 1935, were also reported on in the same issue. Tickets cost the princely sum of 10 shillings and 6 pence.

Other issue from that same year noted that a new cocktail was launched on board the luxury liner *Queen Mary*.

What would working in a London bar have been like in the 1930s and 1940s? Most of the members served in five-star hotels, since there were no pubs or style bars in those days. They were somewhat frowned upon.

The dress code in the city's hotel bars has always been a dinner suit. During the 1920s and 1930s, the style mandated a white drill jacket with black trousers and shoes. In some hotels the lounge waiters continued the wearing of tail coats. The dress code lasted well into the 1950s. Of course, the Savoy's Peter Dorelli spent most of his life in a white drill jacket.

The way of dressing is a bit friendlier now. Business suits have become the accepted norm.

As mentioned earlier, bartenders also were attracted to a life on the ocean waves. The UKBG had an Atlantic branch, which consisted mainly of sea-faring souls who worked for the Union Castle, P & O and Cunard lines.

For these travelling mixologists, *The Bartender* served as a networking vehicle. The same held true seasonal workers who serviced the major resort hotels such as Gleneagles during the summer and in London bars or at one of the 33 British transport hotels like Edinburgh's Caledonian during the winter.

Harry **Craddock** served as president for less than a year. Then Billy Whitfield was elected, serving from 1935 to 1938. Then W J "Jimmy" Tarling, who compiled the *Café Royal Cocktail Book* and *Approved Cocktails* served until he went off to war, in 1940, at which time Billy Whitfield took over again. During its history, the men who donned the heavy silver and gold-embellished chain of office at important occasions, and the International Bartenders' Association annual cocktail competition included EG "Eddie" Clarke, Peter Burbridge, Brian Page, Jim Slavin, G. Quinn, Malcolm Greenall, Peter Dorelli and its President, Salvatore Calabrese.

The **UKBG** played an important role during World War Two. Every member who was called up received parcels from the guild. Freddy Shepherd, who worked at the State Express Cigarette Company, made sure each and every member received an allocation of cigarettes, as well as a copy of *The Bartender* plus a woolly jumper knitted by one of the patriotic women who kept the fires burning at home. There are, in the archives, numerous letters of thanks from UKBG members that were sent while they were serving in Europe and the Middle East.

After the war, some members pushed the motion to create an international organisation—a worldwide fraternity of bartenders. Thus, in 1951, The International Bartenders Association was formed with Jimmy Tarling, the UKBG President as its first President. In 1958, a high point, the IBA roster was about 3500 members strong.

Back in the UK, the guild finally voted, in the 1970s, to admit women. The first woman member, named Rose, worked at London's RAF Club; another was Dorothy Barry from Edinburgh's Hansel Restaurant.

Back in those early days, bartending was seen as a respectable profession. Nowadays, it is more skewed. Some are in the game for the social life, and many aspire to become bar managers or brand ambassadors without formal training. Because of this, at the start of the 21st century, London is the focus of UKBG membership. Members now herald from not only the luxury hotel world, but also from style bars and pubs.

Other things changed since those early days. During the 1930s and even the 1940s, there was a great fear that the UKBG would become a hospitality trade union even though it was always the guild's intention to steer clear of politics.

Its goal continues to be and has always been to train young people in the mysterious ways of the industry. To its credit, the UKBG has run training courses for over 70 years. The training courses have been largely self-financed, although in recent years the UKBG did get some funding from the London Development Agency.

Interestingly, one educational component that existed during 1935 was retired as the number of languages spoken by UK bartenders exponentially increased. French language classes were offered in the afternoons. There currently are too many non-English languages spoken in the trade today for language courses to be offered by the guild.

The UKBG recognizes that the world around it has changed. It is also aware that it needs to change with it. Anyone who goes to one of the National Cocktail Competitions can see that the style bars are now fully represented. And flair bartending has become a fiercely competitive arena on the competition front.

However, history will salute the UKBG for building the solid foundations for a profession that faces many challenges ahead during the current global recession.

Luckily, there is enough experience among its members collectively to make sure the industry will remain in good shape going forward in the future. Stirred, but not shaken.

Hands Around the World

THE INTERNATIONAL BARTENDERS GUILD

BY DOMENICO COSTA

A **conference took place** on the 24th February 1951 at the Grand Hotel in Torquay. Bartender association delegates from a number of European countries decided to create an international association to represent bartenders on a global basis. The subject had already extensively discussed. On that cold wet afternoon, the congress's participants unanimously expressed how happy they were that the proposal, supported by the United Kingdom bartenders Guild, was about to become a reality.

The IBA was set in motion thanks to the association representatives of the United Kingdom, Denmark, Italy, France, Sweden, Switzerland and the Netherlands: WJ Tarling, President of the UKBG; Mr Londahl, President of the Danish Bartenders Guild; Mr Combettes of Amicale des Barmen de France; T Rijken of the Nederlandse Bartenders Club; A Zola of the Associazione Italiana Barmen e Sostenitori; P Melin of the Swedish Bartenders Guild; G Sievi of the Swiss Bartenders Union; and W Roberts of the UKBG.

At that inaugural meeting, the group discussed the formulation of the association's international bartender training programme, elected its first president, and established the initial charter and by-laws of the association.

With this, the IBA took the first steps to set an international standard for making cocktails, whether they are served in London, Sydney, New York or anywhere throughout the world. Nine years later, the IBA met in Paris to determine the best way to classify cocktail recipes by category and designate a select group of recipes as being "IBA approved". Each association was requested to send the most popular recipes for that particular country.

A year later, the IBA approved 50 recipes which were classified as pre-dinner, after dinner, or long drink. Measurements were standardized into fractions and quantities were fixed at 5 cl for short drinks, 7 cl for medium drinks, and 12/15 cl for long drinks.

Training was the next issue to be addressed. By 1966, an open course for young bartenders was launched in Luxembourg under the supervision of Jean Schamburg. A healthy sense of competitiveness and professionalism amongst young IBA members was encouraged when, in 1969, Martini & Rossi expanded the scope of the "Paissa Award" to foreign IBA entrants, not just Italian members, becoming the "International Paissa Prize". This became one of the most important showcases for new talent throughout the world and is now known as the Martini Grand Prix. Ten years later, winning recipes were published in the association's book *50 World Cocktails*.

The beginning of the 1970s saw the IBA grow to 21 affiliated associations with numerous applications being made for membership. (*For a chronology of IBA activities and entry of the various affiliates, see www.mixellany.com.*)

This was also the decade in which the IBA Training Centre found a home in Blackpool, England, thanks to John Whyte, manager of the Hotel and Catering Department of the Blackpool School.

Feminism was a battle cry during that decade. But many association members voted against the inclusion of female members.

Tastes changed and so did expectations during the 1980s. The Educational Development Committee, consisting of Great Britain, Italy, Portugal and Ireland, was established and mandated with the task of producing a study and training program for the IBA Training Centre as well as a correspondence course.

The IBA's list of approved cocktails was revamped to include winning recipes from the International Cocktail Competitions and to delete recipes that were no longer frequently requested by clientele. Measurements were revised to tenths with reference to 7 cl for short drinks, 7 cl for medium drinks and 20 cl for long drinks. In this decade, the "fancy drink" classification was added to the regulations and a "Cocktail of the Year" award was initiated at competitions.

Even though it was still in its infancy in 1999, the "Flair Competition" was added to the competition roster.

Today, there are 53 members associations within the IBA with a total of 42,000 members. And in August 2009, the IBA saluted the 100th anniversary of its oldest association, the Deutsche Barkeeper Union, when its hosted its world-famous international competition in Germany.

Tales
from the Wood

Regarding the Dukes Martini

BY SALAVATORE CALABRESE

I **would like to take the opportunity** to put the record straight about the birth of the Dukes Martini. I was the Bar Manager of the Dukes Hotel bar for over 12 years, beginning in 1982, and I regard those years as the foundation stones of my reputation and career within this industry. Dukes is where I came up with the idea of selling "liquid history", specifically vintage cognac. And Dukes is where I developed a reputation for what I called the Direct Martini as it is made directly in the glass.

This came about, in 1985, when *The San Francisco Chronicle* journalist Stanton Delaplane (who reputedly introduced the Irish Coffee to the United States) used to come to the bar for his usual apéritif as I opened at midday. Famous Grouse on the rocks, then off he would go for lunch. In the afternoon he would return for and ask for his usual Martini in this way: "Salvatore I want it very, very cold and very dry."

I managed to make it cold for him by stirring it longer, but his comment would be "yes it is cold enough but not dry enough". So I would make his second one dry, but he would comment that it was not cold enough. This continued for several days. It became an obsession of mine. How do I satisfy this customer's palette?

One day while I was in the canteen, I observed how others shook the vinegar over their chips. The idea of using the bitter bottle to control how much vermouth is added to the Martini came to me.

The first problem, to control the dryness, was solved. Then I solved the second—the chill factor. I decided to store the glass and the gin in the freezer.

When Mr Delaplane came for his usual Martini, I could not wait for him to try my new method. I began by filling the mixing glass with ice. I then took the glass and the bottle from the freezer. When I saw how cold and dry the glass appeared I decided to dispense with the normal method and poured the frozen gin directly into the glass. I then used the bitter bottle to drop the vermouth on top of the gin and obviously added a twist of lemon.

In this way the aroma and the flavour of the vermouth plays its part throughout the drinking period. I still remember how, as he tasted it, Mr Delaplane's eyes, which were always very heavy, began to lift and light up.

There was no comment!

Then he asked for another, tasted it, again no comment! He walked away. At the time I did not know what to think.

The next day, he came to the bar and introduced himself as a journalist and showed me a piece that he had written for *The San Francisco Chronicle* which described my martini as the best that he had ever tried. This was reinforced by other Martini lovers who sought me out after reading his comments in many publications.

That is how the legend of the Duke's Martini began.

Kingsley Amis, who wrote *Lucky Jim* in 1954, *On Drink* in 1971, and—under the pseudonym Robert Markham—the 1968 James Bond thriller *Colonel Sun*, once commented about my Martini in *The Illustrated London News* that: "We all know how difficult it is to produce not just a well balanced Dry Martini but simply one that stays cold enough without the base recourse to ice cubes in the drink. It was achieved all right."

My good friend Gilberto Preti did not start working for me until 1988 when the Dukes Martini reputation was already well established. Gilberto continued the tradition after my departure from the Dukes, in 1994, with his own indomitable style: A great bartender who deserves all the acclamation he has received.

The Dukes Martini tradition continues with the guiding hand of Allessandro Pallazzi. And long may it last.

EDITOR'S NOTE: One evening after a few cocktails, Salvatore revealed that the secret to the Duke's Martini is dilution. He put the glasses into the freezer wet allowing a little bit of water to freeze inside them.

Is Britain's Capital King?

BY SUE LECKIE

My name is Sue Leckie and I'm a Northerner. And I am fiercely proud of being so. As anyone from that part of England will testify, it also stands to reason that I am biased, not only to my own home territory, but to anyone who has ever been classed as being "regional". You see, us smaller fish like to stick together, defend each other to the hilt, and unite as one when it comes to going up against the big one: in the case of the UK, that would be London .

In the years I have spent in the industry, many of them were taken up being editor of *Theme magazine*. In the days when Simon Difford was penning *Class magazine* (the first time around) declaring it to be the voice of the bartender, and *Flavour* was *Town & Country* (and before its name got all the arrows in it), *Theme* proudly saw itself as the stalwart magazine, focusing on what was happening around the country and not just in London. Now, to be fair, this was partly because we were based in the market town of Stockport while our competitors were rooted down south, and it made it easier for us to flit around the country with relative ease. But is was also because our CEO, Damian Walsh, and our publishing director, Andy Bishop, instilled in all of us from the outset that just because venues weren't based in London it didn't make them bad, it just made them different. And most of all, that these venues were significant, very significant indeed.

If you chart the evolution of the style bar, you'll see that this stance is not just based on local pride, but that it is set down in the history books. Café bar culture, the transition that saw wine bars become independent drinking establishments, began outside of the M25.

Yes, London did have its offerings, but many believe the evolution to have begun in, yes, you've guessed it, Manchester. Its roots began in venues like the Cornerhouse, a stalwart institution that attracted consumers to it because it was different, rather that it just being a place to drink. Additionally, as well as acting as the playground for some of the most inspirational musicians and bands, the city led the way in the world of house music, which had a huge impact on licensed premises, too.

When Factory Records opened the Hacienda in 1982, it didn't take them long to identify that their customers needed a niche pre-club venue that catered specifically for their wants and needs. Step forward the Ben Kelly designed Dry 201, the feeder bar than soon became the stuff of legend. Neighbouring Liverpool soon followed suit with Cream launching sister venue Mellow Mellow. So, the independent style bar, with a new agenda, a new set of priorities and a new client base leapt forth, with many other operators soon opening similar minded venues.

That's not to say that operators outside of the capital have not had their fair share of problems. In fact, there are many additional challenges to be faced, and met, by them if their businesses are to succeed past the launch party hype. First of all there are a few hard realisations: There is not an endless supply of businessmen out on their company credit cards Monday to Friday, nor will the early part of your trading week ever be that busy. Yes, there is passing trade. Yes, there are always those out celebrating, but there are simply not the volumes of drinkers out every day to help guarantee your success. Nor has your customer necessarily been exposed to the more *avant garde* drinking notions, so a more softly, softly approach may need to be taken when penning drinks lists and setting prices.

But many have managed to balance these elements, and have venues that have stood the test of time thanks to their efforts. In fact, some of these very places rank as my favourite places to drink, not just in the UK but in the world. In Northern Ireland, Botanic Inns have opened a plethora of incredible sites, none more impressive than Apartment, which not only competes in terms of looks and cocktails with the best in London, but that also proudly revealed a new confidence in Belfast city centre. In Scotland, Jason Scott and his team have stuck to their beliefs and opened a hugely successful gin bar, Bramble, in Edinburgh, with a second venue on the way. The Northwest boasts the legendary MOJO, where rock 'n' roll meets rum. While in the Midlands, the bar at the Kennilworth has been educating customers and pushing the boundaries of spirits and cocktails for years.

So venues in the regions can justify their credibility, but what about those who work behind the bar? Where are the best bartenders from? In the UK, are the bartenders based in the capital always more advanced, as reputation usually suggests? Or do standards in the regions and, of course, in Scotland, sometimes beat those in the big smoke? Can the geography of the talent in our country be used as a blueprint for the rest of the world?

London undoubtedly is a centre for bartending excellence. Some even see it as the capital of the cocktailing world. There are venues that have become the stuff of legend when it comes to the individuals that have served behind the bars. Match Bar has played home to Dick Bradsell, Tony Conigliaro and a multitude of other talent from Michael Butt and Giles Looker to Sam Jeavons and Pete Kendall. LAB saw Douglas Ankrah, John Gakuru and Myles Davies show the industry just what they had got. At the Sanderson, Ben Pundole, Dan Wilks and Henry Besant served its well-heeled customers.

But take a closer look at those who work in London and you can see there are a great number of bartenders who hail from the regions, and much further beyond too, making London's bartenders more nomadic than born-and-bred capital guys. The capital is a melting pot of cultures, inspirations and trends. Each new settler in the city brings their own style and way of doing things, giving back to the city as well as taking from it.

There are many regional areas that have brought us some of the most heroic individuals. Oxford brought us Angus Winchester, Alex Turner and Kevin Armstrong. Manchester sees Ian Morgan, Beau Myers and Jamie Stephenson ruling the roost, while in the world of flair (and Britain 's Got Talent fame) also honed their skills there, before taking their northern charm to the capital. In Leeds the likes of Gary Hayward, Jake Burger and Mal Evans have ensured that their city has a well-deserved pin on the mixological map. And you would be hard pushed to meet an individual more proud of their Yorkshire roots than *Something for the Weekend* television mixologist and bar owner Andy Pearson.

Other areas strongly celebrate their geographical positioning, and where better than Scotland to demonstrate this. It has a deluge of talented bartenders, a dedicated forum celebrating the art of cocktails in the form of www.barbore.com, several renowned consultancies doing great business, and even a cocktail competition, Liquid Wars, that sees the Scots go head-to-head with the capital in the disciplines of mixology and flair.

So if it's not the venues, nor the bartenders, that suggest the regional offerings are the poor cousins of the capital, perhaps its the city itself that shapes the nature of our bartenders rather than the actual skills they possess. Simon Difford, of *diffordsguide* (and once again now of *Class Magazine*) believes that this, along with the demographics of the consumer, accounts for much of the prowess that is attributed to the London bartender. "Business types with entertainment expense accounts mainly visit larger cities and their influence should not be underestimated. Hence, the world's capitals tend to be where the best bars thrive and where keener bartenders end up," he explains.

Perhaps then, blame partially lies with the consumer and their mindset? "There are simply less people in the suburbs and smaller towns who are prepared, or have the disposable income, to spend on high-end cocktails", says Simon. "The sad fact is there are bartenders in towns up and down the country pulling pints and longing for a customer to challenge their cocktail skills."

Berlin-based Helmut Adam, of *Mixology magazine*, feels this to be a global truth: "It is the capitals that provide enough room for challenging concepts that apply to a special clientele. it is the capitals that are affluent and full of people who like to eat and drink out. It is the capitals that attract innovative people in media, fashion, music and science who inspire us and get inspired by sipping our concoctions."

Then there's the part drinks companies play in the growth and expansion of the industry, and the choice that is offered to the consumer. Most new products launch in the capital, and so those working here have the most ingredients to play with. And it is not just on the spirits front that those in London have more choice. Stores carry a wider range of produce generally and a multitude of specialist stores makes even the most exotic requirement easy to come by.

Gary Regan also points out that larger cities tend to create a fertile breeding ground for new ideas. He explains: "These guys have the chance to learn from each other when they aren't actually behind the stick, and bartenders tend to be generous when it comes to passing knowledge on to others. Bear in mind also that this probably applies to city folk in all trades. The more adventurous move to the big cities."

But is it really that straight forward? Philip Duff, from Amsterdam's Door 74 believes that there are many anomalies globally. "Capital cities can enjoy advantages, but that doesn't mean they automatically lead the pack. Sao Paolo is the place for a drink, not Rio." There are some clear differences in style, too. He continues: "Professional bartending in Holland developed in Rotterdam first, and modern cocktails in Amsterdam, so on the Maas, you'll get great drinks made by bartenders who scoop ice with their fingers and have to jigger everything."

But perhaps the global, regional bartender has an edge. "As far as looking after their customers, and caring for their community though, perhaps it's the small-town bartenders who win out," suggests Gary. "I'm thinking of the guys who drive Fred home after he's had one too many pints, the bartenders who loan Sally twenty quid 'til payday because the rent man's coming. I'm sure this goes on in big cities as well as small towns, but the scale probably leans towards the small-town bartenders in this instance." And isn't hospitality meant to be the principle skill demonstrated by the bartender?

To be honest, should we even be bothered by location at all? Flair-master, Tug Van Den Berg, sums up nicely by concluding: "Bartenders in general, no matter where in the world they are or what kind of bar they work in, contribute in some way or another as long as they take pride in what they are doing. If you find a bartender willing to talk about something they just happen to serve in their specific city, town or country, you listen and enjoy what is on offer. After all, the bartender always knows best."

Can't say fairer than that!

German
Bar Culture

A HISTORY

BY STEFAN GABÁNY

Mixed drinks in Germany became common-
place in the 18th century. The Bischof is mentioned as early as 1775, which was then pre-
pared with red wine instead of port, as it was favoured by the
Bishop of Victorian England. (*See Moses Mendelssohn in* Allge-
meine Deutsche Bibliothek, *1775, Bd. 24, 1. Stück, S. 287-296.*
For the Bishop, compare Cassell's Dictionary of Cooking, *which*
was first published around 1877)

During the 19th century the Bowle [Cup] became a very
popular mixture; it was based mainly on white and sparkling
wine, infused with fruits and herbs: for instance woodruff, which
was used in the popular Maibowle.

The first German books on mixology appeared in 1901. The
J J Weber Verlag published a book called *Bowlen und Pünsche*
on punches based predominantly on wine. Here we also find a

long-time German favourite, the Knickebein: Prepared like a Pousse Café, it is made by topping a liqueur-like cherry brandy with an egg yolk, topped off with another liqueur, like Bénédictine or Kümmel. The book also contains a small section on "American drinks", namely cobblers, cocktails, and sours. They were recommended for breakfasts and early evenings with the caveat: "Beware of German quantities!"

In the same year, Bruno Appelhans published his book *Die Getränke der Gegenwart* [Contemporary Drinks]. Inspired very much by Jerry Thomas' 1887 edition of the *Bar-Tender's Guide* with regard to content as well as design, it contains cocktails such as the Manhattan, the East India, and a Martiné Cocktail [2-3 dashes gum syrup, 2-3 dashes bitters, 1 dash curaçao 1/3 glass Old Tom Gin, 1/2 glass vermouth].

Despite this, cocktails were not common in Germany until the Roaring Twenties, when American-style cocktails and jazz flourished in Berlin just as they did in London and Paris. Alas the party didn't last very long.

The Nazis put an end to "Negro" music and "non-German" drinking habits and during the last years of the Second World War, the few American Bars remaining in Berlin were shut down. (However, there is evidence that cocktails were not completely banned during these dark years: In 1938 Hans Krönlein and F.J.Beutel published their *Getränkebuch* [Book of

Drinks] containing a section with "modern mixed drinks". Then there was a bottled cocktail named Micky Maus, which was produced in 1940. And vintage barware historian Stephen Visakay even claims to own Hitler's cocktail shaker, which allegedly was safeguarded by an US-army officer at Hitlers "Adlerhrost" in Berchtesgaden.

After the war, there was plenty of thirst, but nothing to drink. The liquor industry, which was recovering slowly from the ravages of war, produced inferior imitations of brandy, gin, and whisky: the real stuff being virtually unobtainable due to prohibitive import tariffs. But not even the cheapest quality of spirits could prevent the ambitious German bourgeoisie from indulging their new passion for the American lifestyle and for cocktails in particular. Brandy Alexander, Grasshopper, White Lady, Sidecar, and Gin Fizz were the drinks of the day, despite being on the sweeter side and nothing more than cheap imitations. Creativity in those days was not a virtue that was required in a barman.

Until the early 1980s, the cocktail menus of almost every hotel bar in Germany listed the same drinks—fizzes, cobblers, flips, and the creamy stuff mentioned above—often supplemented by a house "special", usually a concoction of lousy brandy, sparkling wine, curaçao, and Angostura bitters, garnished with a sticky cherry and/or a slice of orange.

Things started to change in the '70s when more and more international products became affordable. With the opening of Harry's New York Bar in Munich, in 1974, Germany saw its first independent bar: a place that was free from the notorious bookkeeping constraints of hotel bars. Pennsylvania-born proprietor Bill Deck appointed Franz Brandl, who was an exceptionally gifted head bartender and one of the first of his guild with a professionally certified training. (Brandl later worked in Eckart Witzigmann's Aubergine, Germany's first three-star-restaurant and published numerous books on mixology including *Gourmet Mix Guide* [Zurich, 1982] and *Brandls Bar Buch* [Stuttgart, 1996]. He also, by the way, supplied a lot of information for the present article.)

Two years later he was followed by Charles Schumann.

As Schumann recalls, when he started out he had nothing more than a couple of his boss's recipes on a Xerox copy and a textbook called *Das Grosse Lehrbuch der Bar* by Harry Schraemli, which was first published in 1943. Schraemli (1904-1995), a Swiss barkeeper, today is regarded as the godfather of German-speaking mixology, not only because of his enormous knowledge, but most notably for establishing bartending as a serious profession in times when working behind the bar was widely attributed to rip-off joints and fraudulent red-light-activities.

What had influenced Schumann most was Schraemli's emphasis on quality. This does not only include the use fresh fruits and top quality spirits—at that time a somehow unreasonable demand for many barmen—but also doing his best to meet the requirements of each individual guest. Schumann's approach to recipes—of improvising and relying on his intuition—together with his hospitality may have contributed to popularizing the pleasures of educated drinking in Germany.

In 1982, Schumann opened his own American Bar in Munich, where he began to create a multitude of recipes, many of which are still popular now. Most notable is the Gimlet, to which he added a few dashes of lemon juice thus turning what is actually a sweet drink into a sour (Schumann's favourite sort of drink). Other popular concoctions are his rum drinks based on what seems to be his passion: combining white and dark rum, for example, in his Leichtmatrose and Rum Runner. (*See Charles Schumann's* American Bar *[New York: Abbeyville, 1995].* This book was published in Germany, in 1991 and is, as far as I know, the first German cocktail manual ever to be translated into English. A part of its success must be attributed to the subtle artwork of Gunther Mattei, an old-time regular, who helped a great deal to develop the public image of Schumann's bar.)

Much to the dismay of Germany's upcoming generation of mixologists, even the Swimming Pool, Schumann's answer to the post-1970s Caribbean craze, is still in high demand. Although he is challenged by youngsters who are returning to the essence and basics of the cocktail and to cuisine-style drinks, Schumann is still highly influential in the bar business, not only in Germany.

From Chícote to the Kalímocho

A CENTURY OF COCKTAILS IN SPAIN

BY ALBERTO GÓMEZ FONT

Probably Mrs Rufina Serrano did not know how to read. Even if she was among the lucky ones who attended school in those days, it is very likely that neither she nor her husband had enough money to buy books of distilled spirits recipes. However, during the years they dated, the years they lived as a married couple, the years they raised their children, a small manual called *El perfecto licorista ó arte de destilar y componer aguardientes y licores* [The perfect liquorist or the art of distillation and preparing spirits and liquors] could be found in the Cuesta Book Shop, in front of the grades of San Felipe el Real in Madrid. The book contained two recipes that could have been used to prepare the mulberry brandy that was sold in the bar next to the Mercado de los Mostenses [Mostenses Market]. One recipe is of mulberry liqueur made by infusion—mulberries previously crushed—in 40 ABV alcohol that was filtered after fifteen days and mixed with sugar dissolved in water from the fountain. The other recipe was mulberry brandy made by distilling the crushed and fermented fruit.

The first job of her child Perico, born in 1899, was serving mulberry spirit to the workers in the market. That child could have not imagined at the time that most part of his life was going to be related to distilled spirits and liqueurs and their combination with other ingredients. He started working to contribute to the family economy out of necessity: his father died when he was only eight years old.

His mother would prepare the distilled spirit and Perico would sell it during the cold Madrid mornings to the wholesalers in the market, who carried the loads away on their shoulders or in their cars to sell on to the street cleaners, to the men in charge of the lamp posts, the greengrocers, butchers, fish dealers, postmen, young men who took care of the loads and to any other regular customers of the tavern on Mostenses Square.

In the summer, he also helped his mother with a small tent she put up to sell barley water and *horchata* (a sweet drink made from tiger nuts and sugar) that she prepared herself.

Before Perico was born, on Amaniel street, not very far away from the square where he worked, the beer factory Mahou was opened. It also had a tavern. It was in this place where our character found his second job, selling peanuts and almonds toasted by his mother. He sold them in a corner of the bar, frequented by a not so common class of drinkers in those times: the beer drinkers.

Next, he delivered telegrams on his bicycle. He was delivery man number 85. Then his means of transport was stolen. He managed to get another, but this too was stolen. (There must have been many bicycle thieves in Madrid at the beginning of the 20th century.) He ended up delivering telegrams on foot.

It did last long before he ended up back in a bar, but a more privileged and elegant place than the previous ones: the bar of the Ritz Hotel where he started as bartender's assistant when he was 17 years old. At a party there, the ambassador of Brazil gave as a present to every bartender and waiter a bottle of cachaça. Perico kept it. This was the first bottle out of a collection that eventually included more than 20,000 bottles. He not only worked as a bartender's assistant at that same hotel. In the gym, he was sparring partner for the Marquis of Portago, a famous race car driver.

Then he had to comply with his duties to the motherland. It was not the best moment for young Spanish men who were called up to serve. There was the war against the rifeños led by Abdelkrim that left thousands dead on both sides.

Young Perico had to go to Africa to fight against people he never knew of and who had caused him no harm. He arrived there as a private. He returned to Spain a sergeant. This title was won through his courage, his services to the homeland and also for the cocktails he served to the officers. While he was there, a while after the sadly infamous disaster of Annual, he was recognized by Gregorio Corrochano, a war correspondent for the *ABC* newspaper who had been his client at the Ritz bar and who immediately informed the leaders of the battalion. Perico went from digging a trench under the enemy's fire to serve Dry Martinis under that same fire of the moor rifles.

It is strange that no movie director has been inspired by this story at least to create some scene or employ the character of a solder serving cocktails to the officers in the battlefield despite the many very good novels, essays, autobiographies that this war generated.

However, my grandfather Andreu Font Aguilá, who also took part in the Rif War did tell me about a soldier from Madrid who was in charge of the field bar visited by the officers and who taught him to serve the vermouth with a piece of orange and a few drops of gin. My grandfather bought oranges for the bar in the marketplace of the friendly *cabilas*.

Many years later and another war, the Korean War, a movie was made called M*A*S*H that was later made into a TV series whose characters were a group of military doctors. In the field operating room, they had a clandestine distillery that allowed them to prepare something similar to the Dry Martini while they played practical jokes on the exuberant woman doctor Morritos Calientes. Outside the screen, though it was a very cinematographic scene as well, equally famous were the 71 Dry Martinis ordered by the war correspondent Ernest Hemingway, when he entered the Hotel Ritz bar with a group of partisans who had taken part in the freedom struggle for the city.

Again in Madrid, in 1923, Perico was in charge of the bar of the recently opened Hotel Savoy. From there he went to the Gran Kursaal of San Sebastian and then back to Madrid to the Cock Bar on Reina Street. Bartending must have paid very well in those times, because in 1925, Perico Chicote bought a bar in San Sebastian where he spent his summers. During the winters he worked in the Bar Pidoux in Madrid. He also had a bar in the Alcázar Theater and another one in La Gran Peña. Six years later, in 1931, he opened the Bar Chicote on the Gran Vía de Madrid (I am lucky enough to live in a house designed by the same architect who built the Bar Chicote: Luis Gutiérrez Soto).

The truth was that Perico held several jobs. Or perhaps he was a businessman because he also ran the bar of Las Cortes (the former parliament of Spain) and the Cock Bar. It was all these jobs that made him leave solid ground and become, for a while, a floating bartender on a series of container ships that carried him to several countries.

Then, the Marquis of Comillas named him honorary bartender for the Transatlantic Company. On the *Ciudad de Toledo*, he was in charge of introducing the wines of Jerez in seventeen American countries.

The first cocktail he created, the Chicote, is a mixture of vermouth, gin, and red label Gran Marnier. Many others followed. Among them the one we could consider as the first well-known case of doping in a bicycle race, which was also a collective doping. It happened in the first edition of Vuelta a España, in 1935, when some bikers drank a cocktail prepared by Perico Chicote to overcome the harshness of some stages. It was a mixture of orange bitter, Gran Marnier, orange curaçao, English gin, and Italian vermouth: a bomb that could be used as rocket fuel for the riders on those heavy bicycles.

Apart from being a fan of cycling, even though his bicycles were stolen when he delivered telegrams, he also liked soccer. He was a supporter of the Real Madrid team, to whom he dedicated the Madrid Fútbol Club cocktail, prepared with half a glass of gin, half of Italian vermouth, a teaspoon of Dubonnet, and some drops of white curaçao. We don't know if the players of that team also used to drink that cocktail before entering the field to score.

Like many great bartenders, Chicote created many cocktails but he never drank any. He did not drink the ones he created nor ones that already existed. He only drank red wine with soda water. He did not like cocktails and did not give much importance to the fact that he could create them, because when he had to explain the requirements for being a good bartender he used to say:

"The most important feature to be a good bartender is to be friendly and generous—but to be genuinely friendly, not fake. And then, to be up-to-date about all the latest events of the country, to be able to follow a conversation about current events, to know always who is fighting a bull, where the next soccer match takes place and what the next big event is. Then, knowing the combination of the beverages in itself is secondary. It is better to know only a few drink mixtures and behave this way than to know ten thousand formulas and be unfriendly and lacking interpersonal skills."

In the basement of his bar in the Gran Vía, he built the beverage museum where he ended up with more than 20,000 bottles from every country in the world. Only once he gave one away as a present to Dr Alexander Fleming.

Once Chicote was dead, José María Ruiz Mateos bought the museum and placed it on the underside of the building of the Banco de Jerez, in Colón square in Madrid. Soon after, with the expropriation of the consortium of Rumasa companies, the Chicote Museum disappeared and the bottle collection was acquired by an individual. For many years now, those bottles have been sleeping in containers deposited in a warehouse outside Madrid.

The bottle that Chicote gave as a present to Dr Fleming, who discovered penicillin, could have been a thank you gift for the money that, indirectly, the scientist helped the bartender earn because in the backroom of his bar this medicine, which could not be found in any drug store, was sold.

That bar, the Chicote, was a weird mixture: a cocktail of illegal trade in products that were lacking after the war, an impressive beverage museum and a bar to meet people. Yes, this was also a place where men could easily have access to feminine companionship among a group a young ladies sitting by the bar.

And there you could also find Ava Gardner, Ernest Hemingway, Luis Miguel Dominguín, Luis Buñuel, or the highest ranking officers of the Francoist government. It was a strange and complex social cocktail that was maybe what turned this bar into a legend.

The legendary singer Carlos Gardel told his friends about his first visit to the bar. At that time, the tango was perceived as the image of a man wailing because he had been deceived by his woman. This is seen in a conversation recalled by the singer: When he arrived for the first time in Madrid, he went to the Chicote Bar where the famous bartender asked him where he came from and what he did. When Gardel replied that he was coming from Argentina and that he sang tangos, the owner asked another question: "And when did your wife leave you?"

If **Chicote** was Madrid's bartender, then a contemporary of his, Miguel Boadas, was Barcelona's. Boadas was born in 1895 in La Habana. He was the son of Catalonian emigrants from Lloret de Mar. He gave his first steps in the tavern run by his parents in the old sector of La Habana, on Calle Del Empedrado [Ed. note: this is the same narrow street where La Bodeguita del Medio would later open]. Since he was a child, he was part of the world of distilled spirits, taverns and drinkers.

Mother and child went back to Spain while the father continued working in Cuba until Miguel turned thirteen and went back to his father's side. Soon after, only two years later, he was already working as a bartender in a bar in La Habana which belonged to his cousin Narcís Sara Parera, a well known member of the Centre Català de l'Havana. At the beginning, the bar was called La Piña de Plata and then it was baptized into La Florida, which later became El Floridita.

There, Miguel Boadas worked as a bartender, and also, as many other great bartenders, he had other jobs because apart from Floridita he sometimes worked in the presidential box of the famous front Jai Alai or in the elegant bar of the Yatch Club of La Habana.

He was thirty-one years old when, in 1925, he decided to come to Spain to visit his family of Lloret de Mar, in the province of Gerona and there he fell in love with a girl called Maria who was later going to become his wife and the mother of his children. This new circumstance in his life made Miguel Boadas contemplate the possibility of staying in Spain. And that is what he did: he settled down in Barcelona and started working in the Moka bar and later in other bars like Nuria, Maison Dorée, and the Canaletas Bar where a special bar was designed and built for Boadas and his assistants.

Finally in 1933, he was able to make the golden dream of many bartenders a reality: opening his own bar. And in October of that same year the Boadas Cocktail Bar was opened, on the Tallers street, a few meters away from the Ramblas, very nearby the Cataluña square.

Now, many years after Miguel Boada passed away, his bar is still a reference point among the people from Barcelona who are fans of cocktails. It is run by his daughter María Dolores, who is always smiling and who has that charm that every good bartender, in this case barwoman, should have with their customers.

The Spanish writer Arturo Pérez Reverte, in one of his novels, *La carta esférica*, places a scene in the Boadas Cocktail Bar:

> "*The woman looked at him curiously. She was smiling a little, perhaps because she was paying attention to the way in which Coy got close to the bar. Instead of staying behind waiting for the bartender to notice him, he moved like a small and compact tow truck among the people that were crowding in front of it. He had ordered a blue gin with tonic for him and a dry martini for her. He brought them back with a skilful pendular like motion of his hands and without spilling a drop. In Boadas, at those hours of the day, that deserved some credit.*»

Also Álvaro Mutis, the Colombian writer who received, in 2002, the Alcalá de Henares the Cervantes Literature Award,

used a character named Maqroll the mastman, who makes several references to cocktails and the Boadas Bar:

> *"Maqroll's problems found a solution in the most unex-
> pected and unpredictable way. One night, in the Boadas
> Bar, where my friend Luis Palomares had requested that
> they take special care of me, I was rehearsing, for the
> umpteenth time, the ideal formula for the dry martini
> when an English man, who was evidently an officer for
> her Majesty in Barcelona, came to me and propose some
> variations that could lead us to the paradigm of that un-
> reachable cocktail."*

To go on now with the list of the cocktail masters of our country would be long and boring, but I
cannot resist naming a few others. I was not lucky
enough to meet Perico Chicote or Miguel Boadas, nor the person who was bartender for the university students from Madrid
during the seventies, the master Ramón Peces, cocktail champion in Spain, who worked behind the bar of the Hotel Tirol in
Madrid, where nowadays they still serve a cocktail called Gallo
[Rooster] that was created by him.

I did meet and enjoyed the last years of Epifanio Vallejo
in the bar of the Hotel Holiday Inn in Madrid and also Eliseo
Ibáñez in the bar of the Hotel Palace. I was also fortunate to be
a customer of the Henry's Bar belonging to my friend Enrique
Bastante, the only Spaniard who has been—with the Mallorca
Cocktail—the world cocktail champion. I even worked face

to face with him one night, in a party for the launching of a magazine in Madrid.

Today, already in the 21st century, I am happy to still be able to enjoy the skill, cordiality and the knowledge of the great masters who appeared during the last century under the baton of Perico Chicote. I am talking about Fernando del Diego who, assisted by his two children runs the beautiful bar that opened a few years ago on the same street and sidewalk as Cock Bar, the first bar of his friend and master.

Furthermore, I also feel obliged to name my great friend Javier de las Muelas, a great bartender and businessman who is to blame for my hobby and fascination for this world. After a few decades of decline—the sixties and seventies—traditional bartending was brought back into life in Barcelona in 1979 by Javier de las Muelas and his Bar Gimlet. It was brought back to life and it was also fashionable. Then other new bars appeared and new professionals until that city became the cocktail reference of our country.

Many others remain unsaid. Some of them I did not meet and many others I did and whose know-how I was lucky to learn and whose company I can still enjoy every time I can find the time to go out and enjoy a drink.

We are also lucky that many of the great bartenders of the 20th century from our country, apart from having left us the heritage of beautiful bars and good recipes, they also explained their work in writing. Let's go over some of those bars and books.

In 1911, a cocktail book was edited for the first time in Spain: *El arte del coktelero moderno: Manera de preparar los cocktails, ponches y demás bebidas exóticas* [The Art of the Modern Bartender: How to prepare cocktails, punch and other exotic drinks], written by Ignacio Domenech in Barcelona.

Later, in 1927, Perico Chicote published the first of his books called *El bar americano en España* [The American Bar in Spain] which contained a prologue written by the journalist Gregorio Corrochano, the one that stopped him from digging trenches and start serving cocktails in the African war. He wrote the following:

> "One afternoon on May 1922, he was encamping a column in the Jemis de Beni Arós. The walk had been a bit tiring. [...]. At war, where what is needed the most is not to be needed, and you barely eat, you barely sleep and you barely live, sometimes all of a sudden appear those capricious cravings... and the man that sometimes survives without anything is obsessed with refinement and he suffers for it [...]. That afternoon in Beni Arós, one from the column wanted to drink a cocktail. Only to mutter the sentence sounded like a dream caught up in the mysteries that flow from the tombs of Muely Abdesalam. With the obstinacy of a drinker, he found a soldier that knew how to prepare a cocktail. He was an engineer soldier called Perico. That Perico, an unsuspected bartender in the abstemious valley of Beni Arós, has today his throne in Madrid."

The next was the book of Pedro Talavera, who was bartender in the Hotel Palace. In the introduction of his manual called just *Cock-Tails*, the author gives us this curious piece of advice:

> "*A piece of advice: if one wants to drink well one should go to the bar accompanied by a beautiful woman. Or two. It is not that if one goes alone is not going to drink well; but if he brings company he drinks better because, I don't know why, when the bartender sees beautiful women he shakes the cocktail shaker faster and more energetically*".

Later two books from Jacinto Sanfeliu called *Cien cócteles y El bar* [One Hundred Cocktails and The Bar] and *Evolución y arte del coktail* [Cocktail Evolution and Art] appeared. Sanfeliu worked in the Palace, the Ritz, and in the Pasapoga dance-hall, until in 1955, he opened his own bar in Madrid called Balmoral. Even today this bar remains as one of the best cocktail places of the city thanks to the mastery and charm of Agustín Nieva and Manolo Herrero, the current owners and bartenders.

And in the meantime, Perico Chicote also continued writing cocktails books: *El bar americano en España* [The American Bar in Spain], *La ley mojada, Mis 500 cocktails* [The Wet Law, My 500 cocktails], *Cocktails mundiales* [World Cocktails] and *El mundo bebe* [The World Drinks], this last containing illustrations by Antonio Mingote. In some of these books, Chicote includes this great decalogue for the bartender:

1. Respect and love the client above all things.

2. Never call him by his name unless he expressly authorizes so.

3. Honour his tastes.

4. Honour him in its presence or absence.

5. Do not let him drink in excess.

6. Do not bother him or ignore him.

7. Only charge him for what he drinks.

8. When speaking about him, say only what is necessary and accurate.

9. Do not wish for love whims he may have.

10. Do not envy his position or comfort.

Fernando Gaviria, who had a bar in La Habana another one in San Sebastián and two others in Madrid, very close to the one belonging to Chicote on Víctor Hugo Street and on Reina Street, published in 1954 a little book (to give as a present to his clients) called *La cátedra del gin fizz* [The gin fizz chair]. And, in order of appearance, the list goes on with the books by Juan

Palenque: *Combinados especiales de fruta o moderna cocktelería española* [Special fruit mixtures or modern Spanish cocktails], Epifanio Vallejo: *Manual del barman* [Bartender's Manual], Jesús Felipe Gallego, Armando Carranza, and José María Gotarda, the unforgettable bartender from Barcelona that prepared delicious cocktails in the Bar Ideal and whose son is following the family tradition.

In the introduction of *El gran libro de los cocktails* [The Great Book of Cocktails], Gotarda says that speaking of cocktails is the same as drinking in company, and he adds: "Even if someone is alone and orders a cocktail in a bar, there exists always communication between the two. This know-how and making conversation are essential features of a good bartender or a good host".

And the list goes on with the book by Manuel Pedraza, and the one from María Dolores Boadas, who compiled her father's recipes in a beautiful book published for the 50th anniversary of her bar. Then the book from Ángel Jiménez, good friend of mine, called *Del Palace a Balmoral, Memorias de un barman: De los 40 a los 90* [From the Palace to Balmoral, A Bartender's Memoirs: From the '40s to the '90s] where the author describes his experiences since he started working in the bar of the Hotel Palace until he retired as director of the Balmoral.

Also waiting to be edited as a book are a bartender's memoirs that, together with a collection of more than three thousand recipes, are under the title *El universo de la coctelería y memorias de un bartender: Más de tres mil cócteles)* [The Cocktails Universe and the memoirs of a bartender: More than three thousand cocktails]. Joaquín Grau, the author, was born in Alcoy a few months before the beginning of the Spanish Civil War. When he was eighteen years old he emigrated to Venezuela and there, he developed his bartender career until 1995 when he came back to Spain. He was twice champion in Venezuela and now he gives bartender's courses in Alicante and Benidorm.

There are also three thousand cocktails in the most complete of the so-far published books called *El práctico de la cocktelería: Resumen mundial del cóctel* [The cocktail practice: World summary of the cocktail] whose author is Antonio Comas, a bartender from Mallorca. In this long collection of recipes there are at least two with names that evoke these islands: the Canary cocktail and the Guanche cocktail.

So far that is the list of books written by bartenders but there is also another list: the list about the cocktail books written by professionals and specialists of the hotel industry who have not worked behind a bar: *Aperitivos, cocktails y refrescos* [Aperitifs, cocktails and beverages] by Carmen S De Sans; *El bar en casa* [The Bar at home] by Martínez Llopis; the extremely famous and reprinted book by Carlos Delgado *365+1 cócteles* [365 + 1 cocktails]; *el Manual práctico de Coctelería* [The Practical Manual of Cocktails] by Martine Beaulieu, a Canadian living in Spain; *Cócteles y combinados* [Cocktails and combinations] by Félix Grande, and, lastly, the beautiful book by the cinema director

Luis Garci called *Beber de cine* [Cinema drinks], which is the compilation of ten articles published by the newspaper *ABC* in which the author explains the story and anecdotes of ten cocktails relating them with the cinematographic world. I would like to give some special attention to this beautiful fragment from the epilogue of this book:

> "...the bar is already closed, but the bartender is kind and let us finish off, with calm and laziness, the penultimate drink, while he finishes making calculations in a corner, or reads the newspaper or fills in a bet slip. It is nice to be laying on the leather couch, drink at hand and be able to clearly contemplate– that is one of the big miracles of alcohol – that thing that is sometimes so difficult to see: life."

Moreover, the very one that is now talking to you has written a cocktail book. It is called *Cócteles Tangerinos* [Tangier Cocktails] and it is a collection of ten stories that take place in the Tangier during the years following the Second World War. The main character is the bartender from the Hotel El Minzah and in every story there is a cocktail created by him. Furthermore, a few years ago I was requested to create a list of cocktails with Havana Club Rum for El Guadarnés bar of the Hotel Hacienda Benazuza, near Sevilla.

And Javier de las Muelas, the bartender and businessman from Barcelona about whom I was talking before, came up with the idea of asking a few friends to write a short story or poem where they spoke about the dry martini. With that material, in 1999 a beautiful book was published called *29 Dry Martinis (That's the limit)*, where there appear twenty-nine short stories by twenty-nine authors. I feel honoured to be one of them.

We are on the island of Tenerife, and here, in its capital, I had years ago the opportunity to enjoy the perfect and meticulous service offered by the bartenders of the Hotel Mencey. And when I found out that my first conference about cocktails was going to be here I started to look for references of cocktails related with these islands and I could find what I believe is the only book completely dedicated to Canary cocktails. The book is called *Cócteles con miel de palma de la Gomera* [Cocktails with Palm Honey from la Gomera], and its author is Manuel Mora Morales. And I also was lucky to find on the internet the recipe of a cocktail called Folía de ron canario y Vichy Catalán whose author is José María Gotarda from the Ideal Cocktail Bar from Barcelona. The ingredients are: 1/2 lime juice (green lemon), 6 cl honey rum Arehucas, 1 teaspoon cane sugar, mint, and Vichy Catalán sparkling water.

Later, during the 1970s, the Hawaiian and Polynesian bars came onto scene. This happened at a time when the only good places to drink cocktails were very few bars like Chicote, Ranea, Gitanillos, and Balmoral in Madrid, Boadas and El Ideal in Barcelona, Ricardo in Málaga, El Corzo in Salamanca apart from the big hotel's bars where good bartending was continuously practised. The Hawaiian and Polynesian bars appeared first in

Madrid and Barcelona and later in other cities and some towns on the seaside from which the tourism industry survives.

Those were places, some of them are still there, with a decoration that would transport us to far away beaches with tropical plants, ponds with colourful fishes, waterfalls on the wall and furniture made of bamboo. When you enter the bar you are received by people wearing paper Hawaiian necklaces. This exotic presentation was also present in the cocktails, served in coconut or pineapple containers, volcanoes, wizard masks, and full of small paper parasols, lighted sparklers and even special effects like the smoke made with dry ice. And let's not forget about the names of those delicious drinks: Tangaroa, Coco pae pae, Hula hula, "Sueño de verano" [Summer's dream], "La cueva del dragon" [The dragon's cave], "Ruiseñor de Konga" [Konga's mockingbird], Wahine…

Sometimes during Easter, I still visit one of those bars, the Pay-Pay in Sitges where, given that I am friends with the owners, they let me prepare the Dry Martinis we drink before dinner.

Many people at that time also preferred to use the word "*combinado*" [another Spanish word for cocktail] to refer to those exotic mixtures. Years before, the word "*combinación*" was used in Spain as a translation for the term "cocktail". For us, the Spaniards, the pronunciation of the word "cocktail" is a "*paroxitone*" [a word with a second-to-last syllable stress] and for the Hispano-Americans is an "*oxytone*" [a word with a final syllable stress].

Even today in some hotels they offer some cocktails or *combinaciones* that are difficult to find. An example of this would be the Gran Hotel de Salamanca where in the cocktails list. we can find two drinks hard to find in cocktail recipe books: *media combinación* [the half combination] and the *ginebra preparada* [prepared gin]. In that bar, where the stockbreeders from the Campo Charro get together to talk about their bulls and their bullfighting, I asked the bartender, while drinking a well done dry martini, about those two drinks and he explained me how he prepared them:

MEDIA COMBINACIÓN
In the cocktail shaker put 1 part gin, 1 part red vermouth, 1 trickle of curaçao and some drops of Angostura (or another bitters).

Ginebra preparada
1 glass of gin, 1 sugar lump, 1 piece of lemon skin and sparkling water.

The *media combinación* is also served in Lhardy, the oldest pastry shop of Madrid, where after I ordered the drink from one of the employees, he went into the office and a while later came out with a small tray with a small glass that contained an ice-cube, a piece of orange skin, another of lemon skin and a dark amber colour liquid, which is the result of mixing red vermouth, gin and triple sec.

Ángel Jiménez, in one of the chapters of his book *Del Palace a Balmoral*, when he describes how the habit of drinking cocktails was introduced in Spain, explains that at the end of the 1940s and beginning of the 1950s, drinks like the Gin Fizz, Dry Martini, and the Media Combinación were already considered as fashionable. And then he adds: "The product that was used the most to prepare these mixtures was the gin that could also be drunk just with ice and sparkling water".

In the book by Fernando Gaviria there is also a cocktail called Combinación and its ingredients are: 3 parts of red vermouth, 1 part of gin, drops of curaçao, drops of Angostura, mint leaves, two cherries, a piece of lemon, and a piece of orange. This same recipe can be found, with small variations, in Chicote's books as *combinación cubana* [Cuban combination].

I **have spoken** about bartenders, bars, and books, always placing the cocktail in special and exclusive places. But there are also popular cocktails, created by the people and drank in common bars and taverns or at outdoor parties. Let's think for example about the Queimada Gallega and the Cremat Català which both clearly have Cuban influence. And following that same line of hot drinks we have to mention the Carajillo, the true Carajillo, that is only coffee with a trickle of any liquor, which can be rum, anisette or brandy.

Furthermore, the Revuelto drank by the people from Zaragosa must be considered as a cocktail as well. These are known in Cataluña and Valencia as Barreja or Barrejat and contain a part of muscatel wine and another part of Cazalla liquor. And if those are popular cocktails, we cannot forget about the Pomada de Menorca which is a beverage drank by the countrymen from the island and that consists of mixing natural lemonade with local gin, also known as *ginet*. No, I don't forget the most famous one, the one that tourists drink while laying in the sun eating paella: our refreshing Sangría.

I have told you about three scenes where cocktails and military uniforms appeared together: Perico Chicote serving the high ranking officials in the Rif War; the TV series called M*A*S*H, where the characters were military and prepared something similar to the Dry Martini with the surgical instruments from the field hospital and the arrival of the liberators of Paris, during the Second War World, with Hemingway, in the bar of the Hotel Ritz.

Now I will tell you the fourth story, one where I was the protagonist in 1979, when I was sergeant of the Department of Transmission Engineers, in the Academy of Engineers of Hoyo de Manzanares. One afternoon, I was sitting there talking to some soldiers of my battalion and one of them offered me a one litre Coca-Cola bottle and said:

"Have some Kalimocho, sir."

"Some what?" I asked with curiosity.

"Kalimocho, sir. You never tried it?"

"Well, no, never. What is it?"

"Coke with red wine, sir."

The look in my eyes must have been so terrible that the poor soldier put the bottle away and passed it over to one of his colleagues.

The Kalimocho, that horrible mixture, at least to me, did not appear in my life until many years later, in 1997, and very far away from that place. This time it was in Venezuela, in a little town called El Hatillo, close to Caracas. I went there to have dinner with some friends and later they decided to take me for a drink to a bar that belonged to Basque people. Finding compatriots that own a bar so far away from home is always fun and one feels like talking to them, but that moment was ruined when the person in charge of the bar offered us a typical cocktail from Spain... Yes, exactly that: the Kalimocho. Obviously, even there, I did not try it. I decided instead to mix the Coca-Cola with a good rum from the country.

The anonymous author of that mixture—I resist to call it a cocktail—could have never imagined how successful he was going to be and even less, the amount of times the name of his drink was going to appear on the pages of the newspapers. It has been significant the trouble caused by the Botellón in the big and not-so-big cities. I could see this happening live in Cáceres. And when speaking about this social phenomenon you also wonder what the young people drink when they get together in the parks to spend the night drinking, or better said, getting drunk.

A little while ago, in the Sunday supplement of the newspaper *El País*, an interview about the Botellón was published and there appeared a short glossary of the terms used to refer to the street drinking mixtures. To the cry of "*Hidalgo! Hijoputa el que deje algo!*" [Hidalgo! Motherfucker the one that does not finish!] that indicates that you need to drink the content at once from huge glasses, the young people drink the following:

- **Kalimocho/Kalimotxo**. Coca-Cola with red wine in equal parts. According to some internet websites dedicated to this beverage, in order for the Kalimocho to taste good, the cola beverage has to be the best, that is to say Coca-Cola; whereas the red wine has to be the worst, the cheapest and of course one that comes packed in a box.

- **Kaligorri**. Coca-Cola with rosé.

- **Kalitxurri**. Coca-Cola with white wine.

- **Pitilingorri**. Lemon Fanta with red wine.

- **Txurrimuski**. Orange Fanta with red wine

- **Rebujito**. Seven-Up with dry sherry or manzanilla.

If the above-mentioned mixtures turn out to be too light, you can opt for something stronger, like mixing Coca-Cola with red wine, vodka, and rum: Superkalimocho, or something like this must be the name of this mixture. A bit sweeter, but not less stronger is the one known as Cua-cua, the result of mixing Cointreau with Licor 43.

Mixing wine with water has always been the sin of the bartenders. Mixing it with sparkling water was the way to get a refreshing drink for the hot Spanish summers. And we saw that this one was also Perico Chicote's favourite drink. Later, much later, another mixture arrived, the mixture of red wine with fizzy lemonade, and some decided to call it Tinto de Verano [Summer Red Wine]. I am one of those who believe that mixing wine with anything is a crime, but there are lesser crimes, like mixing it with sparkling water and other more serious crimes would be to add soft drinks, and even much more serious would be the Kalimocho.

Chicote was friends with many politicians and if he lived today and could still visit them, he probably would repeat a phrase that may seem like a premonition of the problems alcohol would cause to the young people from our country. Mr Perico used to say: "I think nobody should be allowed to drink alcohol until they finish school and started working. If I were a statesman I would create a universal law about this."

It finishes here, with my total refusal to drink a Kalimocho. But before I finish, I would like to take two more steps, one backwards and the other towards the future.

Long before Miguel Boadas and Perico Chicote were born, at the beginning of the 19th century, in 1806, the Catalonians Pedro Font and Francisco Juncadella built a building in New Orleans to be used as housing and as a warehouse for the foodstuff imported from Spain (among them red wines from the Priorato and sherry wines). Soon after, in 1815, a nephew of Mrs Juncadella called Aleix turned the ground floor of the building into a coffee place and named it Aleix Coffee House. And there, in that coffee place, in 1874, the Catalonian bartender Cayetano Ferrer created a cocktail, Absinthe Frappe, that became so fashionable that they decided to change the name of the bar into The Absinthe House. That bar is still open and a new addition has been made to the name: The Old Absinthe House, and they still serve the cocktail created in United States of America by a Spanish bartender from the 19th century.

Now, at the beginning of the 21st century, the creators are still working. Cocktails have found their way into the laboratories belonging to the greatest chefs, the daring chefs, who with traditional recipes create new presentations and obtain new textures. A while ago, the bartender and journalist Juan Luis Recio, that every Sunday publishes an article about cocktails in the magazine *El Semanal*, told us that the chef Ferran Adriá created a cocktail for an ophthalmologists congress that took place in San Sebastián. The cocktail was served in the Kursaal (Perico Chicote worked there) and it was a green-coloured Daiquirí named Visudyne, in which the liquid and the foam are made apart: this last with one of the already famous siphons from the Catalonian cooker. And it was something similar that I drank the last time I had dinner in Madrid, in the restaurant La Terraza del Casino where the kitchen is run by Ferrán Adriá.

When we sat down, while we were reading the menu (from which we understood only half) we were served some small glasses with Gin Fizz; but it was Gin Fizz with warm foam and cold liquid… delicious, a peek into the future of cocktails. And there, in the Casino de Madrid, behind the beautiful bar of the bar Las Estancias, there is another professional and friend: Ángel San José, abstemious bartender that never stops searching for new combinations.

To wrap it up, let's go back to the phrase of Perico Chicote that I read a few minutes ago: "I think nobody should be allowed to drink alcohol until they finished school and started working. If I were a statesman I would create a universal law about this."

Well, clearly I and the rest of the people that are now here have completed our education and already started working, so, I propose we make a toast, even if it is just a symbolic one, for being lucky enough to be here. And what can be better than doing so with a cocktail. I dare to propose a new cocktail to you. One that is inspired in a fragment from the book of José María

Gotarda, from the chapter called *Un nombre para un cóctel* [A name for a cocktail]:

> "*A client in a bar orders:*
> *—One martini; nine parts of gin and one of ver-mouth.*
> *—Good, Sir. Do you want a lemon twist?*
> *—Hey! — the client says balefully—, I have not or-dered a lemonade.*
> *This story can lead to a new name for a cocktail, for instance, martini lemon*".

So, I believe from that last paragraph we can grasp the main concept and create a new drink. Let's put in the cocktail shaker some Canary white rum and let's add a trickle of dry vermouth and some drops of Canary banana liquor. After cooling it we pour it in a cocktail glass with a piece of ripe banana. And then the organizers of this gathering will be in charge of giving this new cocktail, which is now your cocktail, a name.

What's in the Bottle

The Seductive Spirit

BY CAIRBRY HILL

The world over, Cognac is recognised as the most coveted, expensive, seductive, luxurious, indulgent and sophisticated of spirits. So how did this most coveted of spirits achieve this legendary status? One would be forgiven for thinking that Cognac must be the result of hundreds of years of gentle nurture and care, and whilst this is certainly true it is far from the whole story. War, religion, taxation, plague, famine, and disease have all played their part, not to mention a generous helping of the noble pursuits of smuggling, piracy, and a serious amount of adultery and womanising.

Choosing when to start the history of Cognac is a challenge in itself. Ultimately it started somewhere between 135 million and 65 million years ago, during the cretaceous period. At this time the Cognac region we know today lay beneath a warm, shallow sea inhabited by billions upon billions of microscopic plants and animals. As these micro-organisms died their tiny calcitic skeletal structures fell to the seabed. Over millions of years limestone deposits were laid down, creating the soils that define this region today.

Grape cultivation however came along some time later and was introduced to the region by the Romans during the 2nd century, although at this time there was no such place with the name Cognac.

Wine-making in the region thrived under Roman rule. However, it was rudely interrupted by the Germanic Vandals and other tribes, in the year 406 when they ripped through the region evicting the Romans.

The Vandals didn't stay long and were replaced a decade later by the Visigoths. Despite this turmoil and bloodshed the vines and the wine-making capability of the region survived and flourished.

Soon enough another bunch of invaders took control – the Franks headed by their leader Clovis ruled the region they named Aquitaine. Under Clovis much of the administration of the region was passed to the bishops and monasteries they founded. At this time we find the first records of wine export from the region to Flanders and Britain.

Unfortunately this was not sustained by Clovis's descendants and Aquitaine descended into chaos until the close of the 600s. Plague, famine, and Frankish raiders all played their part. The wine industry in the Charente region did not really develop further until 800 when Charlemagne became emperor of the Frankish empire.

Then came the Vikings. By 840 bounty raids escalated into full on invasions and whole areas of the Charente and beyond were regularly sacked. For generations the region was in a state of flux with control passing from one warlord to another.

It was not until the 11th and 12th centuries and the rise of the Benedictine movement that things got back on track. Monasteries, abbeys and churches started to appear everywhere and reshaped the landscape. This coincided with a period of excellent weather that would last almost 200 years. At this time the town of Cognac was best known as a centre for salt trading for the interior of France. Salt was shipped up the Charente from La Rochelle establishing this trade route and enriching the local lords through the taxes they collected. La Rochelle became the main commercial port for the region, exporting wines and salt all over Northern Europe

In 1137 the fifteen-year-old daughter of Guillaume X duke of Aquitaine, Eleanor (Alienor) of Aquitaine, began a hectic journey to power following her father's death. Within three months she was married to Louis son of Louis VI. Just a month later, following the death of Louis VI she became queen of France. However in 1152 the marriage was annulled, so two months later she married Henry Plantagenet heir to the English throne. When he became King in 1154, Alienor became queen of England. Naturally trade between the region and England flourished and indeed also across much of northern Europe.

Alienor's son John did his best to undo all of this. In 1200, whilst attempting to forge a peace treaty with the count of La Marche, Hugues IX de Lusignan, John decided to make things interesting by sending Hugues to England on business and marrying his fiancé Isabelle whilst he was away. Enraged, Hugues turned to the French sovereign Philippe II Auguste, who sided with him and ordered the confiscation of all John's lands in France. He managed to lose nearly everything apart from the port of La Rochelle and a small piece of Aquitaine. He spent the much of the rest of his life trying to regain lost lands amid endless partying. In 1215 he reportedly placed an order for nearly 110,000 litres of Gascony clairet (quite a thirst).

When John died, his wife Isabelle returned to her home of Angouleme where she married Hugues X de Lusignan the son of the man she had originally been engaged to. The couple would have a significant impact on the future of the region. Firstly they helped pave the way for Louis VIII to seize the port of La Rochelle, severing the wine trade with England. Then, in 1241 when Alphonse, the younger brother of the new king Louis IX was granted control of the region, Isabelle inspired her husband to lead a revolt against the Capetian rulers. Henry III of England on hearing news of this revolt decided to take advantage and sent an army to try and capitalise on the ensuing chaos. However Louis IX reacted quickly and Henry was ultimately defeated.

Isabelle and Hugues were to pay a heavy price, though spared their lives they lost much of their lands and ultimately marked the end of this family's role in the history of the region.

Whilst still squabbling, Louis and Henry kept themselves occupied with bouts of ill health and the odd crusade before they eventually signed the Treaty of Paris in 1259. Unfortunately, this proved to be an unworkable arrangement. Whilst Henry renounced his rights to much of France, it left him with Aquitaine and it stated that if Louis's brother Alphonse died leaving no heir, his lands south of the Charente would also revert to England.

This is exactly what happened when he died in 1271. By 1286, half of Cognac country reverted to English rule. This was not by any means a comfortable arrangement and there was a great deal of conflict between English and Norman sailors in the region. By 1294, the region was plunged into war again. It was quickly realised by both sides that this was a war neither side could win and peace returned without resolution. The region then enjoyed a brief boom time during which wine production and exports soared, it lasted until 1315 when those 200 years of fine weather came to an abrupt end.

A **very dark era** descended upon the region, but it was not just atmospheric. Known as the Hundred Years War, the fighting actually rumbled on for longer. War between the English and French was almost continuous throughout the region for much of the 14th century, this combined with the impact of the black death, decimated the population, in fact by 1445 the total population of France had fallen to 10 million—half the number a century earlier. During the 14th century wine-making in the Cognac region was almost nonexistent. From deliberate destruction and simple neglect the vines across the region were wiped out.

Things did not improve much with the dawn of the 15th century. Civil war now became intertwined in the conflict between the French and English and plague continued to play its part. By the 1420s to 1430s Aquitaine was also being ravaged by bandits.

The Hundred Years War ended 17 July 1453 at Castillon. The French finally regained control of the region which had been ruled by the English for nearly 300 years, though it had been all but destroyed.

Peace quickly brought prosperity and by the end of the 15th century the cognac region was experiencing a rebirth. The whole of France in fact was in the throws of the first Renaissance and it is likely that in this time of exploration and learning the first eau-de-vie was produced in the Cognac region. Distillation and the use of alembic stills had been known in France for centuries in apothecaries, producing medicines but the first record of a reference to a brandy fit for international trade is dated 1517 when a "barrique d'eau ardent" was shipped from Bordeaux. The earliest reference to eaux-de-vie being shipped from La Rochelle is dated 1549 and by 1571 we have the first reference to a "merchand et faizeur d'eau-de-vie" a man by the name of Jehan Serazin. He is believed to be one of the first local distillers of eaux-de-vie in the Charente region.

Around this time the name "brandy" was also coined. Understandably, the drink had become popular with English and Scandinavian sailors, and its root is the Dutch word *brandewijn* meaning burnt [distilled] wine.

By the 17th century, numerous Dutch agents had begun to settle in the Charente region, bringing with them their Scandinavian copper pot stills. Brandies from Cognac were starting to be recognised for their quality. In 1617, the first bill of sale with a guarantee that the brandy had been produced in Cognac appeared in La Rochelle. The secret to this superior quality lay in the nature of the wines produced in the region. The wine was of such high acidity that it was perfectly suited to distillation. In fact, an excellent drinkable spirit could be achieved after just two distillations or *chauffes*. Brandies from other regions required many more rectification stages in order to produce a brandy of equivalent quality, however this resulted in brandies which lacked the flavour that the Cognac brandies were able to retain.

I n **1624,** there is a record of two Dutchmen, Van Der Boogvert and Loo Dewijk building a distillery in Tonnay-Charente. And in 1638 an English traveller; Lewes Roberts wrote of "a small wine called Rotchell, but more properly Cogniacke."

Dutch influence in the shaping of the region was further demonstrated when Philippe Augier de Chateuneuf married into the Dutch Jansen paper-making family who were based in Cognac. He was persuaded to move to Cognac where he established the Augier trading house, one of the very first Cognac trading houses.

One of the biggest stresses on Cognac producers during this time was the burden of taxation. This was the time of the Thirty Years War and the war was funded by taxes. This burden was dealt with in a number of innovative ways. The simplest and most direct method involved armies of peasants known as *croquants* sweeping across the countryside. Whenever they encountered tax collectors, they were swiftly put to death in time-honoured spectacular fashion. One favoured technique was to strip captured officials naked, tie them to a board and them beat them to death with batons and small hammers (they really seemed to dislike the tax collectors).

The other and less literal method of beating the tax man was through smuggling. Taxation between neighbouring towns, could vary greatly. Therefore, the incentive to transport Cognac between towns undetected was obvious.

But it was avoidance of taxes in foreign markets (especially England) that lead to the creation of a thriving smuggling industry that would be responsible for the creation of some of the great Cognac houses we still know today.

Just as cognac was taxed domestically in France to help fund conflicts, exportation and importation taxes in England were equally punitive, and for largely the same reasons.

The Channel Islands, free of taxation, became a crucial staging post for smugglers targeting the south west of England. It was from here that Jean Martell learned his trade. Born in Jersey in 1694, Martell's first venture in the world of Cognac was as a smuggler. By the start of the 18th century, smuggling had grown into a big business. However, Martell's future lay in production rather than smuggling Cognac. In 1715, he moved to Cognac and established a successful and legal trading house, trading a variety of items such as groceries, seeds, and knitted goods. Martell also married into two of Cognac's leading brandy-producing families. Martell himself entered the trade, at first exporting non-aged brandies, and by the early 1720s his company was shipping more than 40,000 barrels each year. Germany was an important early market for the company, although by then England was already Martell's top customer. It was at this time that smuggling into England was reaching its peak, hitting a level in 1719 which would have been unimaginable five years earlier. One week in

October of that year, there were two runs of unprecedented size: one at Worbarrow Bay on the Purbeck coast, the other further west near Bridport. The run at Worbarrow involved no less than five ships unloading simultaneously and an observer described "a perfect fair at the waterside, some buying of goods and others loading of horses; that there was an army of people, armed and in disguise, as many in number as he thought might be usually at Dorchester fair, and that all the officers in the county were not sufficient to oppose them." In the Bridport run, a great quantity of brandy and salt was brought ashore and "carried off by great numbers of the country people" in full view of the customs staff. In all likelihood a consignment of salt and brandy would have originated in the Charente region.

During the 1720s, Cognac exports were given a shot in the arm thanks to the disastrous financial crisis attributed to John Law, the Scottish economist whose policies had dominated France's finances since 1715. The result was a devaluation of the French currency, which greatly favoured expensive exports such as Cognac.

This period was also significant as it was during the 1720s that the first rough roots of delimitation of the cognac region started to appear. Those Cognacs made within about 15 kilometers of the town of Cognac were given the highest marks and referred to as Champagne eaux-de-vie. Cognacs from around Saint-Jean-d'Angely in the northwest corner of what is now the Fins Bois were named Best Cognac. A third area considered of

lesser quality lay west and south of Fins Bois in the area now referred to as Bons Bois. A fourth area running up to the Atlantic
coast around La Rochelle and Rochefort produced eaux-de-vie
that was not even referred to as Cognac as it is now and roughly
corresponded to the Bois Ordinaire.

By the time Jean Martell died in 1753, his company had
become the dominant player in the region. But this decade and
the next were to see a number of significant new players come
onto the market: first Gautier in 1755, followed by James Delamain in 1759, and then Richard Hennessey in 1765.

James Delamain was an Irish Protestant from
Dublin. He was one of many Irishman who had seen
the boom in cognac in Ireland and wanted a piece of
the action. He formed an allegiance with a major local trader,
Jean-Issac Ranson who was looking for a toehold in the Irish
market. As was often the case in Cognac, the family relationship was forged before the business relationship—in this case
when Delamain married Ranson's daughter in 1772. That same
year the two men formed Ranson and Delamain in Jarnac. In
no time at all they had replaced Martell as the main supplier of
the Irish market.

A few miles inland from the English town of Bridport in
Dorset you find the town of Beaminster. Its most famous son
was Thomas Hine, who would eventually give his name to Hine
Cognac. Thomas was born in 1775, into a family who reportedly

had numerous and strong links with the smuggling trade. It was likely that this is how he developed his interest in cognac and at the age of nineteen left Dorset to seek his fortune in France. He found employment in a brandy business in Jarnac. However this was the time of the revolution and Thomas being a foreigner was suspected of being a spy. He was imprisoned in Chateau de Jarnac where he was to meet a befriend another imprisoned, foreign cognac trader Richard Hennessey. Both Gentlemen were however fortunate that it was none other than James Delamain who was in charge of the Jarnac police and who therefore had responsibility for the two prisoners. Delamain eventually arranged for the two men's release and even invited Hine to his house. There he met Delamain's daughter, Françoise Elizabeth who in 1797 he married. For Thomas Hine marrying into the Delamain family instantly made him a player in the market working for Ranson Delamain. In 1817 he took over the running of the company and changed its name to Thomas Hine & Co.

The period between 1800 and 1807 was mini boom for the Cognac region with exports rising from 32,000 hectolitres 100,000 hectolitres, but this was not to last. In 1804, Napoleon became Emperor of France. Following the Battle of Trafalgar in 1805, he imposed the Continental blockade which, combined with further elevated import duties imposed by the English, had a devastating effect on the Cognac industry. By 1808 exports had dropped back to 55,000 hectolitres eventually falling to a low of just 16,500 hectolitres by 1812. A number of cognac houses managed to just keep afloat during this period by supplying brandy to Napoleon's armies. Courvoisier in particular have made their association with Napoleon a cornerstone of their marketing for centuries. It was, however, the house of Sazerac de Forge & Fils that he turned to when he asked for the creation of a cognac to celebrate the birth of his son, Napoleon Francis Joseph Charles in 1811. This cognac was to bear his son's title Roi de Rome —The King of Rome.

It was conscription that was to have the most damaging effects of Napoleons rule: the demand for horses, fodder weighed heavily on Charentaise farmers and conscientious objectors were dealt with harshly (as many as 16,000 were imprisoned on Ile de Re where hundreds died as a result of disease or execution). By the time of Napoleon's defeat in 1815, there were few Cognac traders who were unhappy to see the back of him.

Whilst the first third of the 19th century had been hard (the weather had between 1816 and 1820 was terrible), there were some benefits. As a result of the Napoleonic blockade vast stores of cognac had been ageing away in cellars, maturing to ages not normally allowed. During this time a significant number of cognac houses appeared on the scene, including Exshaw (1805), Croizet (1805), Salignac (1809), Menard (1815), Marange (1815), Hine (1817), Chabasse (1818), Bisquit (1819), Marnier

(1817), Renault (1835), and Godet (1838). There were an equal number that didn't survive these years.

Cognac exports to the main English market suffered due to import tariffs until 1940, when the British Parliament imposed a sharp 30 percent cut in the tariff applied to cognac. The effect was instantaneous: Cognac exports soared to 200,000 hectolitres by 1849. Other areas of the French economy did not fair so well during this period and elections in December 1848 brought Louis Napoleon Bonaparte to power. The second empire was a law-and -order regime but also a pro-business one. Financial stability and then momentum grew in the Cognac region.

The year 1858 saw the first attempt at delimitation of the Cognac vineyard regions. A map was produced by a Charentais geologist, Henri Coquand dividing the region into four crus: Grande Champagne, Petite Champagne, Premiere Bois, and Deuxieme Bois.

What was so significant was the manner in which the map was constructed. All previous maps had been based on the geographical convenience of trading towns. Coquand not only based his map on the nature of the rock, subsoil, and topsoil he found, but he also employed the services of an official taster to assess the qualities of the eaux-de-vie they sampled across the entire region. His map drew a clear link between the *terroir* and the style and quality of the eaux-de-vie it ultimately produced.

The 1860s were a boom time for Cognac. This was largely due to the hero of the 1840 tariff reduction, Richard Cobden. The signing of the Cobden-Chevalier accord cut tariffs on Cognac by half whilst raising tariffs on English domestic spirits. For the first time Cognac was trading on an equal footing.

Planting of vineyards expanded and grape cultivation techniques advanced, with vines now being grown in uniform rows on wires. By 1870, the area planted with vines in the region had hit 243,000 hectares (the size of Luxembourg). A second map of the region was produced in 1870 and now included the Fin Bois and Bon Bois Regions.

1870 marked a turning point. Over-production had forced cognac prices down by 20%, but this was nothing compared to what would result from the discovery in 1872 of a tiny root louse, *phylloxera vastatrix*, which had the ability to destroy vineyards with incredible efficiency

In 1872, the cognac vineyard stretched from the Atlantic coast through the Charente valley to Perigord and totalled 246,000 hectares. Phylloxera did not go to work instantly however, vine planting continued to expand reaching a maximum of 283,000 hectares in 1877, but this was short-lived. By 1893, the vineyards of Cognac had been annihilated, and only 41,000 hectares remained.

The louse had been introduced on the rootstock of native American vines transported to Europe as experimental grape varieties. The French government, initially slow to react, upon realising the severity of the problem offered a huge reward for whomever could find a solution to the Phelloxera problem.

Ultimately the solution lay in the source of the problem. A French horticulturalist Gaston Bazille suggested that as it was the louse attacking the root systems of the French vines that was killing them, American vines must have a natural resistance to this attack. Therefore in theory a French vine grafted onto an American root stock may have a natural resistance to Phelloxera. The hunt was on for the ideal rootstock vine combination. This task was passed to a young viticulture professor by the name of Pierre Viala. He travelled with a fellow plant expert Frank Lamson-Scribner of the United States Department of Agricuture to the US where they discovered the combination of hybridised root stocks that would eventually solve the problem of phylloxera. By 1888, the vineyards of Cognac were being replanted, but it was a long slow process. By 1895 the Cognac vineyards still only totalled 55,000 hectares. Progress was slowed by more unwanted American introductions. The first was a fungus called downy mildew that decimated grape crops. Then a second fungus called black rot arrived. At the end of the 19th century, Cognac's greatest challenge was how to meet the growing demand for their product with the limited supply. This gap between demand and supply was starting to be filled by fakers from all corners of the world. There are reports that by the end of the century Italy was exporting fifty times more fake Cognac than it was importing of the real thing, not to mention Russian Koniak and Spanish Coñac to name but a few.

The Cognac houses had only one choice, they had to go to work to protect their terrain. The first step was a massive increase in the distillation capacity of the region. The major houses built new distilleries to help fill the shortfall in supply. There was also a move from the use of the traditional Folle Blanc grape that when grafted had a susceptibility to rot. It was replaced with the Ugni Blanc grape variety.

The hierarchy of classification was also born at this time, with the designations VS, VSOP, XO, and Napoleon being defined.

However, the key step taken to defend Cognac in the riotous market of unsavoury "fake" brandies was the 1909 government decree defining the Cognac zone. This declaration stated that an eaux-de-vie could only be called Cognac, if it had been distilled within the specific geographical area that it described. The map that was used was the same map defined by Henri Coquand in 1870 and was thus ratified by this ruling.

And Other Things

Exposition Universelle des Vins et Spiritueux

BY ANISTATIA MILLER & JARED BROWN

It **is a collection** of over 8000 bottles of wines dating back to 1834 and spirits to 1811, thousands of wine and spirits labels, well over a thousand menus from around the world, nearly 600 pieces of glassware, vintage distillation books and equipment as well as history and recipe books related to drinks, wine, and spirits. Exposition Universelle des Vins et Spiritueux is the world's largest, oldest, and most comprehensive museum of its kind that is open to the public.

Situated along the Côte d'Azur in France is a unique island that stands as a monument to a man, his vision, and the unique industry to which he devoted his life: Île de Bendor. On this private island Paul Ricard erected a museum dedicated to housing a "complete encyclopaedia" of wine and spirits, Exposition Universelle des Vins et Spiritueux.

A visit to this island and its museum is more like a pilgrimage than a weekend getaway. It is a little more than an hour's drive from Marseille and a couple of hours from St. Tropez. Once you arrive in Bandol, you take a short ferry boat from the harbour. Upon debarking, you find yourself transported to a world that lies somewhere between Mediterranean fishing village and a French-version of Portmerion, Wales—the backdrop for the 1960s British television series *The Prisoner*. You can clearly see why French comedian Fernandel, artist Pablo Picasso, pop legend Johnn Halliday, oceanographer Jacques Cousteau, and cosmonaut Yuri Gragarin gravitated to Île de Bendor. The museum looks over two small beaches that attract thousands of sun worshippers each and every year: a curiosity nestled between two beachside cafés and a sailboarding school.

To understand why this museum exists and its significance, you must become acquainted not only with the history of the island and the man who built it, but with the important role that France and particularly southern France has played in the development of the world's alcoholic beverages and mixed drinks throughout history.

The History of Île de Bendor

In **1950**, Paul Ricard attended a dinner party in Bandol at a house overlooking a barren island—rock unbroken by trees, and marked by an ancient wall built to repel Saracen invaders back in the 8th century. Looking out to sea from the terrace he decided to buy the island and to return to his first passion by creating an artists' colony, beginning with a monolithic tribute to Puget, bearing the motto "Nul Bien Sans Pein" which stands today at the entrance to the Hotel Delos. Within two years he had built the island's first hotel, restaurant, bar, artists' studios, and galleries.

Artists visiting Île de Bendor during the 1950s and 1960s were provided with extensive facilities including an ironworks where much of the island's ornamental ironwork was created, and a glassworks with a giant glass oven next to the beach.

Here, elegant pieces were created for collectors from around the world, including New York's Waldorf-Astoria Hotel and Metropolitan Museum of Art. The styles created ranged from classic Spanish tableware as many of the glassblowers arrived from Spain to acid-etched cameo works that were frequently mistaken for and as highly-prized as those of the great Art Nouveau glassmaker Emile Gallé.

The glassworks were located on Ile de Bendor until the 1960s when the oven was turned off and a new one was constructed near Paul Ricard's Formula One racetrack in Le Castellet.

Île de Bendor was a popular destination for celebrities during the 1960s. A frequent guest was comedian Fernandel, who became a close friend of Paul Ricard. He starred and narrated a documentary about the island in 1965 titled Nul Bien Sans Pein. Ricard's interest in film was not just a personal one. He produced a number of films himself, including Calact and the pirate film Barbarosa.

The island was also home to the first color television studio in France, housed on top of the cinema in the central gardens.

The EUVS Building

Designed and built, in 1958, by Paul Ricard the EUVS building was intended to be a cathedral to the world's wines and spirits. On 12 July, Paul Ricard and a group of his esteemed colleagues from the industry presided over the opening.

Ricard wanted the French people to be able to see what was happening in the rest of the world as well as around France. His vision was a collection that would be "permanent, eternal, and ever growing." To this end he even constructed the building to support three additional storeys, though at this time we are more interested in expanding through the internet to share the collection with the entire world.

Beginning in January 2007, a three-year-long program to rejuvenate this treasure was launched. The entire collection was removed from the building and catalogued in both documentation and photography. Under our direction the entire collection was sorted into research and exhibition collections the task of identifying, cataloguing in both documentation and photography, and analysing each item began. Employing the latest in reversible conservation techniques, items were treated and stored to preserve and extend their life for viewing by future generations researchers and the general public.

The next year, the building itself was given a facelift. Essential maintenance was only the beginning. Lights were installed throughout the museum for the first time in its existence. The frescoes that adorn the interior were cleaned and restored. UV coated windows were installed to protect the collection from damaging ultraviolet light.

A small exhibition entitled, "France and the World of Drink", was installed in the island's Galérie, that summer, which was also EUVS's 50th anniversary. Many new acquisitions and items placed on loan to EUVS were added to enhance the museum's scope and to fulfill its mission.

During the summer of 2009, the EUVS building was completed and a new exhibition was set in place. But the EUVS also entered the 21st century, when its website was redesigned by Upian in Paris and relaunched in June. With this, the world's "complete encyclopaedia" of the wine and spirits industry dedicates itself to educating and entertaining new generations of visitors to Île de Bendor and to the global village of the internet.

The Art of EUVS

The **EUVS building** itself testifies to the influence that wine and spirits have on the fine arts. The statues of Bacchus and Vigne, which guard the entry to EUVS were carved by the famed Provençale artist Louis Botinelly (1883-1962). The ceramics which decorate the façade were executed out by Mirielle Ginard and Henri Couve.

The fresco "The Warriors' Wine" was executed by Milanese artist Gianni Bursamolino (born in 1928). Bursamolino had been invited to work in France in 1956 by Paul Ricard and Pablo Picasso. The following year, he worked with Paul Ricard to launch an art competition that invited young students to create the other EUVS frescos. (His works were later exhibited in the Gallery on Île de Bendor next to Salvador Dali's "Tunafishing", the Surrealist master's largest work.)

Approximately 500 square meters were devoted to the competition winners. Among the young artists—aged between 17 and 22 years—involved in this project were Raymond Hurtu (born 1935) of Nancy, Danièle Bonnet of Avignon, Roger Remy of Rouen, Albert Martin of Aix-en-Provence, Michele Dolfi-Mabily of Toulon, Michael Martin of Angers, Alain Bailhache (born 1937) and D'Orvale of the National School of Decorative Arts in Paris. At the time of the inauguration of EUVS, three of these young talents received an additional Jury Prize for their work. Hurtu received 100,000 francs for "The New Wine", Bonnet and Remy accepted 50,000 francs for their frescos.

The Entry Foyer

From the early 1950s to the 1970s there was an artisanal glassworks, Verrerie de Bendor, housed on the island. This was part of the artists' colony Paul Ricard created. As a young man, Ricard's first dream was to be an artist, and though his father pressed him to make his fortune in the beverages business, he never lost his passion or his talent for art.

The first works produced in the artisanal glassworks were all of a distinctively Spanish style. The glassware made of bubbled glass, which is created by adding sodium bicarbonate to the molten glass, is one of those early styles. The Spanish influence was logical: the first glassblowers employed on the island came from Spain.

Later, a young glassblower arrived on the island with a passion for the work of Emile Gallé, one of the most famous French glass artists at the turn of the 20th century. He bought a broken Gallé lampshade and studied it until he could replicate Gallé's work. Then he made the style his own. Works like his from Verrerie de Bendor were collected by the Louvre, the Metropolitan Museum of Art in New York, and scores of galleries in Europe and the United States. (There are rumours that some unscrupulous gallerists removed the Bendor signature from some pieces and replaced it with Gallé to raise the value.)

Paul Ricard also founded Céramiques Ricard, which produced a variety of functional and sculptural ceramics. These are still prized discoveries in antique shops throughout the region.

The Art of the Menu

The menus in the table displays are from an international collection of 1200 restaurant and drink menus dating from the 1860s to the 1960s. They were discovered, in 2007, by the director/curators in one of the refrigerators of a disused boucherie here on the island. We are not sure who assembled the collection and it was only discovered it when refrigerators were being cleaned to be used during the conservation process.

There is a first class menu from the first Air France flight from Paris to Tokyo. There is a typewritten menu from the Georges V in Paris that was presented at a banquet, in 1947, held for the then-new prime minister of India, Pandit Nehru. There is a banquet menu created and hand-signed by Salvador Dali for the Hotel Meurice in Paris. There are menus from tiny village restaurants that were each original watercolour paintings made for one night only. There are diplomatic dinners from various embassies around Europe. It was customary for someone to draw the table on the back and pass it around so each attendee could sign at their place.

The menu collection is being digitized so that they can be viewed without damage from environment and human contact.

Cocktail and Wine Books

EUVS has acquired a collection of books on subjects ranging from cocktails to distillation to wines. Some of the highlights include *Bariana*, the second oldest known French language cocktail book, *Cocktails de Paris*, from the 1920s, and another outstanding French cocktail book Frank Newman's *American-Bar*. These books and others are now available for free digital download via the EUVS website. This is another facet of the EUVS mission: to put the knowledge into the hands of anyone who is interested in the information contained in EUVS no matter where in the world they are.

Cocktail Tools
and Harry's New York Bar

The modern bar spoon, an essential tool for every bartender, evolved from the French medical spoon. This spoon had a precisely measured bowl. On the other end was a muddler for crushing pills and crystals into powders. The handle was twisted to facilitate stirring. The only real difference between the modern bar spoon and the only French pharmacists used in the 18th century is the length. Modern bar spoons are a bit longer. (There are examples on display in EUVS near the books.)

The bars of Paris were legendary for their cocktails from the 1860s to the 1930s. This art is returning to Paris once again. A few places from that time never closed their doors. Harry's New York Bar is perhaps the most famous of these.

By the early 1900s, cocktails and mixed drinks had become of a staple of daily social life. Every major metropolis had scores of hotel bars, cafés, taverns, and cocktail bars. Originally owned by famed American racing jockey Tod Sloane The New York Bar opened its doors in 1911 at 5 Rue Daunou in Paris .

Famed among locals as well as avant-garde artists and writers who flooded Paris from the United States, England, Germany, and Russia, the bar was purchased from its original owners by Scottish barman Harry MacElhone in 1923. Among the classic cocktails invented by MacElhone and barman Fernand "Pete" Petiot at what became known as Harry's New York Bar are: the White Lady, the 75, French 75 (after absinthe was banned in France), Bloody Mary, and Monkey's Gland.

That same period saw the invention of the Rose cocktail at the Chatham Bar also on Rue Daunou around 1922, the Mimosa at the Ritz in 1925, the Sidecar at Henry's on Rue Volney and more.

Despite the enactment of prohibition in the United States during the 1920s and into the 1930s, cocktails thrived in France at places such as Harry's New Bar and their creativity influenced the world decades later.

There is also a new generation of bars on the leading edge of the Parisian cocktail Renaissance. Bars such as Experimental Cocktail Club, Curio Parlor, and Mama Shelter are reaching back to the Golden Age of Parisian cocktails and building on that foundation to reach new plateaus. Though this trend is just beginning, these bars and their barmen are already receiving much deserved international recognition. On any night these bars are sure to be filled with people from around the world who have arrived for the new French cocktail experience.

The Entry Alcove

Despite the international cocktail boom during the early 20th century, pastis was still the preferred French apéritif, especially in the summertime and especially in southern France where it had long been the drink of locals and holidaymakers. Pastis time was a welcome moment in the day when people gathered to discuss politics, current events, literature, art, just about anything. This was the observation of young Paul Ricard, who worked in his father's wine business in Marseilles while studying art.

After release from military service, Ricard attempted to set up his own line of table wines, then brandies. While selling his products to local bars, he came to an epiphany: "The popularity of pastis made its mark on me. I wondered quite seriously whether it would be a good idea to develop a product which would satisfy the taste of all those pastis lovers, to take over the whole market, a market which did not even have to be created, since it was already there."

In 1932, Ricard and his brother began produce and market his personal creation—Ricard, real Marseilles pastis—with a loan of 600 litres of alcohol and money to purchase a second-hand still, a stock of bottles and three alcohol vats from former absinthe-producer Pernod.

The overwhelming reception the product received throughout southern France and Catalonia in its first year was beyond the dreams of the young aspiring artist, who by the 1940s became one of world's most influential liquor producers.

The "Cube" represents a broad, but not complete, selection of the products in the Pernod-Ricard brands family as it was in 2008. It was contributed to the EUVS collection on the occasion of the museum's 50th anniversary. The museum, we should note is supported privately by the Ricard family and still receives donations of bottles from around the world to be preserved here for future generations.

French Spirits Alcove

The vast majority of the world's liqueurs and cordials are French, have French origins, or were inspired by French products. Just read the labels on the back of the bar, and you will find crème de cacao, orange curacao, triple sec, Cointreau, Grand Marnier, crème de menthe, cassis, and many other products labeled with French names no matter where in the world they are produced and consumed.

One French creation lured international celebrities from royalty to writers to scientists to politicians: Vin Tonique Mariani, a fortified Bordeaux wine infused with coca leaves. French chemist Angelo Mariani invented the tonic in 1863. Not many alcoholic beverages could boast a Vatican Gold Medal. But Mariani's could. Pope Leo XIII and Pope Saint Pius X thought the elixir was as beneficial tonics for the body, brain, and nerves. So did influential people who happily offered 16 printed volumes of their endorsements as testament to its popularity.

From its invention, competitors try to grab a portion of Mariani's amazing success including Dr. John Pemberton of Atlanta, Georgia, who created Pemberton's French Wine Coca in 1885. Less than a year after he went to market, prohibition was enacted in the city, forcing him to redevelop his recipe without the use of wine. Thus, Coca-Cola was invented.

Vin Tonique Mariani, Elixir de Combier (developed in 1834 by Jean-Baptiste Combier who also invented Triple Sec) and Liqueur Raspail (developed in 1847 by chemist François-Vincent Raspail) were the three most famous "health-giving" spirits of the day. Mariani died in 1914, two years before the United States enacted legislation against unprescribed tonics such as Mariani's. His secret recipe died with him.

The French style of making drinks in the 19th century was different than the American style. In United States, bartenders would produce elaborate concoctions for customers from a great number of bottles behind the bar. The French style allowed the bartender to appear more relaxed when working, because much of the work would be done days, weeks, or months before the drink was served. Ratafia is a good example of this, as are fruit eaux-de-vie, and pastis.

One reason cocktails became so popular in France was the onset of the phylloxera plague, which began its decimation of the French wine industry around 1862. Almost overnight, cocktails became part of the daily fare along with an elixir that was consumed not only in cocktails but on its own: absinthe.

Abram-Louis Perrenoud scribbled a recipe for extrait d'absinthe in his diary around 1794. Major Dubied purchased the recipe four years later and produced it under the name Dubied Père et Fils with Perrenoud's son Henri-Louis as chief distiller. In 1805, Perrenoud changed his surname to Pernod and established his own absinthe distillery—Pernod Fils—which continued producing absinthe until the First World War.

That is when pressure from temperance groups and wine-makers' associations coupled with the well-publicized 1905 Absinthe Murders fuelled a ban on the "Green Fairy" in France in 1915. The nation's absinthe producers quickly changed their recipes, creating anise-flavoured spirits such as pastis that would appease the public.

Spirits of the World Alcove

istillation began in China and the knowledge was traded along the silk road to India. It reached Egypt with one of Alexander the Great's generals who became Pharoah Ptolemy I. The word itself doesn't come from the Egyptian word *"khol"*, which is antimony distilled into a powder for eye makeup, but comes from the Arabic word *"al-khol"*, meaning the genie that comes from the bottle or that which takes away the mind.

Distillation traces its western history from the University of Montpellier in the 13th century, and spread to Britain, Germany, Spain, Ireland, and the New World from there.

French alchemist Arnaud de Ville-Neuve (1235-1311) was the first European to document the distillation of wine for consumption. He is also credited with coining the phrases *"aqua vitae"* and *"eau-de-vie"*.

A professor at both the University of Montpellier and the Sorbonne, de Ville-Neuve proclaimed that he had discovered the long-sought universal panacea that prolonged life. According to some historians, de Ville-Neuve was also the father of vin doux naturel, the process of adding spirits to wine to halt fermentation and preserve sweetness, which is sometimes called mutage. But it is his discovery of aqua vitae that triggered the creation of four classic French spirits: armagnac, cognac, marc, and eau-de-vie.

When he died in 1311, he was not sainted. In fact, at one point the Church labelled him a heretic as he had taught medicine at a time when many people believed doctors were tampering with God's work. However, his daughter became a nun and was canonized after her death. She is Saint Rosalie.

Here you can also sample some of the ingredients used to make spirits. While the next room describes the distillation process in depth, here you have:

Peat cut from a peat bog on Islay, an island off the west coast of Scotland that is famous for the strong peaty taste of its whiskies. Islay is home to eight distilleries: Caol Ila, Bruichladdich, Bowmore, Lagavulin, Laphroaig, Kilchoman, Bunnahabhain, and Ardbeg.

The peat flavour comes from malting the grain. This process starts with sprouting the barley by wetting it and then spreading it out on a warm floor for about six days. As the grain sprouts, the carbohydrates are broken down into sugars that provide easy food for the yeast during fermentation. The sprouting is stopped by toasting the grain over a fire made of burning peat blocks. It is here that the distinctive smoky flavor comes into the whisky. Peat is simply vegetation that died and was compressed over a long period of time in an environment that prevented it from completely decaying. It burns like coal and was once used to heat major cities like London. (London fog came from peat smoke not humidity.)

The barrel stave comes from the Laphroaig distillery, though like all Scotch whisky barrels it was used first in the United States to produce American whiskey. Under Scottish law, all whisky produced in Scotland must be aged for a minimum of three years in used barrels. Barrels play an important part in the production of aged spirits and wines.

If you look closely at the side of the stave you can see how far the liquid inside penetrated the wood during warm weather. When it is cold, liquid inside a barrel contracts out of the wood, drawing many flavours with it. When a barrel is charred inside like this one was, it contains approximately 135 different flavour compounds, including six or seven vanillins alone. Toasting the barrel also creates caramel flavors from the naturally occurring sugars in the wood. Charcoal does not just add flavour. It also acts as a molecular filter. The structure of the carbon atoms make them receptive to bonding with volatile compounds that make wines and spirits taste sharp, bitter, or harsh. Before a barrel is re-used it is often "re-charged" by burning it again or at least heating it. This removes the unwanted flavours from the charcoal, activating it once again.

The juniper berries here come from the Beefeater distillery, which has been produced in London since 1820. Juniper has been used in distilled spirits since as early as 1055 AD in Salerno, Italy. However, juniper gained immense popularity during the plague years of the 14th century. To ward off the bad odors they thought caused the plague, doctors wore masks filled with juniper, people wore juniper necklaces, draped their homes with juniper garlands, planted juniper hedges, used juniper as a seasoning in their foods, bathed in it, covered themselves in juniper oil, and drank it in many different drinks. They did not know why juniper worked. They simply knew it kept them alive and that was all that mattered to them.

Here at EUVS we recently discovered why juniper was effective at warding off the plague. The answer is surprisingly simple: Juniper is an effective flea repellent, and the plague was spread by parasites in fleas.

The grains on the pedestal are Russian wheat and barley, used to produce vodka. There are approximately 1,000 distilleries producing 100 recognized brands of vodka in Russia.

The bottle containing the viper is placed in a cabinet with Asian products as there is a long tradition of placing snakes in bottles of spirits in southeast Asia, especially, Vietnam. It is part of Oriental medicine. Snakes are widely believed to possess medicinal qualities and the wine is often advertised to cure everything from farsightedness to hair loss, as well as to increase sexual performance.

However, we believe this particular bottle is French or Swiss in origin. There is also a tradition of serving snake wine in the alps region. Shepherds caught the snakes to keep them from biting their sheep. Then the snakes were positioned in the bottle, which was filled with eau-de-vie. Needless to say, drinking snake wine is more a rite of passage than a culinary pleasure. The production of snake wine was banned in France in the late 1970s.

The large urn behind the snake wine is a mao-tai container from China (circa 1820). Mao-tai, the largest selling spirit in China, is made from sorghum, a plant similar to sugar cane.

More of the world's distilled spirits are produced from sugar cane than any other fermentable substance. Sugar cane comes from the South Pacific. The Chinese discovered and imported it. Then they introduced it throughout Asia. Alexander the Great was one of the first Europeans to encounter sugar cane and remarked about "honey from the reeds". Genoese merchants brought sugar cane to Europe. It was brought to the New World around 1500ad, where it was destined to become the raw material for aguardiente, aguardente, rhum, ron, rum, rhum agricole, and cachaca.

In Mexico, a succulent desert plant called the agave is used to produce mescal and tequila. The plant takes eight to ten years to mature. Then the spikes are cut off, and the center portion, the piña, is roasted, ground up, fermented and distilled. The piña is surprisingly sweet once it is roasted and was an important part of the natives' diet for centuries. It was originally thought that the Spanish conquistadors introduced distillation to Mexico. New evidence indicates that there might have been earlier Chinese or Fillipino explorers. Traditional native distillation methods and stills are closer in style to Asian than European. Today, tequila is a tightly controlled appellation. Only agave spirits produced in Mexico's mountainous Jalisco region are legally called tequila.

The American Revolution was fought over taxes on alcohol production. Yet, when the first American president, George Washington took office, he imposed a tax on whiskey to fund construction of the White House. The Whiskey Rebellion of 1782 was so widespread, nearly as many troops were called to fight as had fought against the British. The whiskey distillers were mostly Scots-Irish immigrants who had first settled in Massachusetts, then moved to Pennsylvania for the fertile soil, longer growing season and pure water. When the troops approached, many of them decided to move to the western frontier: Tennessee and Kentucky. Here they discovered that wheat and barley did not grow as well. However, they found corn to be an excellent substitute. Thus, Kentucky Bourbon and Tennessee whiskey were born. When President Washington retired, he began distilling whiskey on his farm in Virginia. Fortunately for him, his successor Thomas Jefferson repealed the whiskey tax.

Spirits Production Alcove

The fundamentals of spirits production have not changed since the beginning. To make distilled spirits you ferment something: making a basic wine or beer. The Mongols used mare's milk. The Russians used beets. Honey was historically popular, but is a bit too expensive these days.

The fermented liquid is then slowly heated. Alcohol boils at a lower temperature than water, so the steam that rises contains different quantities of alcohol at different stages of the heating process. It also contains many other compounds. The first steam contains highly toxic chemicals. One early monk experimenting with distillation remarked: "Do not stand in front of the still when the steam is rising or you will drop dead as so many monks have before you."

The middle part or heart of the distillation contains the highest concentration of beverage alcohol. It is very difficult to separate this from other substances such as isopropyl alcohol, which comes off the still at almost the same temperature. This is why many products today go through multiple distillations. But this is part of the distiller's art as too many distillations strip desirable flavours from the spirit as well as bad ones.

The steam is condensed back into liquid by cooling it. This is done by directing it through a long pipe that coils through cold water. To keep the water cold enough it is allowed to flow in and out of the still, constantly replaced with fresh cold water.

Filtration is the next step of spirits production. There are two types of filtration: particulate and charcoal. Particulate filtration removes any solids, anything that might be floating around in the spirit. Charcoal filtration has a similar effect to barrel aging as it smoothes the flavour of the distillate by removing sharp, volatile flavours.

Vodka is relatively simple to produce (though making high quality vodka is an art). To make vodka, grain or potatoes (or any other fermentable substance) is made into a beer. This is placed in a still, distilled, and filtered. The pure spirit is combined with water to bring the strength down to a drinkable level. Then it is bottled.

Most gin begins with neutral spirit, which is produced in exactly the same fashion as vodka. The spirit is then combined with botanicals. Juniper must be the predominant flavour, but gin makers use a wide variety of other natural flavours: bitter or sweet orange peel, lemon peel, angelica root, orris root (the root of the iris flower), licorice, cardamom, cinnamon, cassia, cubeb berries, coriander, and nutmeg are just a few of the common ingredients.

In the 1800s Bordeaux was a major gin-producing region. Brands like Old Peter's Gin, Pickwick's Gin, and Suze Gin were common throughout France at this time.

The small still on the upper shelf in the center display is a Salleron Dujardin alembic still that was once very common in France both for producing eaux-de-vie at home and for producing perfume essences. Although many of these stills are well over 100 years old you can find them still in use across the country.

On the bottom shelf is a new alembic in a very old style. This is the type of still used by the Moorish and early European alchemists. These stills can be purchased from a number of sources, though they are more often used for decoration than distillation.

The large still in the back of the alcove is a model of a giant wooden rum still that is still in use today at the Demerara distillery in Uitvlugt, Guyana. It is a mid-1800s Savalle column still.

There has long been a debate as to whether vodka was born in Russia or Poland. The earliest use of the word appears in a Polish book published in 1534. This book also refers to a book from 1405 about vodka in Poland. Russian historians claim that vodka was invented there in 1410. However, most written records from that time have been lost or destroyed so the final answer to this question may never be found.

Cognac Alcove

Distilled twice in Charentais pot stills and aged in Limousin oak barrels, this grape eau-de-vie has been produced since the early 1600s in the Cognac region, one of three demarcated brandy regions in Europe. Cognac was so popular during the 1700s and 1800s, that to commemorate the birth of Napoleon's son, the King of Rome, a special batch of cognac known as Roi du Rome was bottled in 1811.

After the Second World War, a new style of cognac was marketed by a handful producers for making long drinks—spirit served with soda and ice.

But cognac is not the only French brandy.

Arnaud de Ville-Neuve is often credited with inventing, in the 1300s, armagnac—an aged grape eau-de-vie that was originally consumed for its health giving properties. Given its designation on 25 May 1909, armagnac is produced in an *alambique Armagnalais*, a specialized type of column still, and aged in Limousin oak barrels. Within the Armagnac region there are three production zones, Ténarèze, Haut-Armagnac, and Bas-Armagnac.

According to some historians, Lord de Gouberville was the first to produce, in 1554, an apple eau-de-vie distilled and aged in the cognac style in Charentais pot stills. Produced primarily in Normandy, calvados is called *eau-de-vie de marc de cidre*, if it is distilled from apple cider instead of apple juice. This eau-de-vie experienced a "golden age" when the phylloxera plague devastated France's vineyards in the 1860s.

Distilled from the leftover solids of grapes pressed for wine, marc or eau-de-vie de marc is a French pomace brandy produced a style similar to Italian grappa. Most grape-growing districts in France produce a marc. The best-known examples come from Burgundy, Romanée-Conti, Musigny, Chambertin, Nuits-Saint-Georges, Meursault, Auvergne, and Montrachet. The most expensive is Marc des Hospices de Beaune and the lightest is Marc de Champagne.

The Altar

The fresco above the stage is an interesting portrayal of the Last Supper. Only Christ's hands appear: one holding a glass of wine and the other extended in friendship.

Inside the cabinets are original statuettes created by Henri Couve, representing the heads of the wine associations who supported EUVS when it first opened. Today the museum is honoured to maintain close relationships with these groups.

The centre display holds a statue of Saint Vincent, patron saint of wine growers. In his hand is a serpette, a traditional vineyard tool. Nearby is a bottle of 1834 vintage Turckheim wine from Alsace, a region on the border between France and

Germany that has changed hands between the two countries five times in the past 136 years. The region is well known for Gewuztraminer—a name that is often misinterpreted as meaning perfumed, but really means aromatic. This 1834 bottle is the oldest wine in the collection. Next to it are very early bottles of Ricard, and an 1811 Roi du Rome Cognac created to celebrate the birth of Napoleon's son whose title at birth was the Roi du Rome.

The doors on the cabinet were closed and locked for at least 25 years. No one on the island could remember ever seeing the cabinets open. So when they were finally opened again, in 2007, it was like a time capsule. On the left side were thousands of wine and spirits labels mounted on stiff paper that had never been placed on bottles. Some of the labels were prototypes for products that were never produced.

The next cabinet contained thousands of pieces of museum stationery and blank menus bearing a logo that had not seen before that was almost identical to the new logo that the director/curators were designing for EUVS. The next contained hundreds of photographs from the 1960s of parties in the museum and on the island. The last cabinet had a small sign inside: "*enfer*". Here they found wines produced outside appellations but bearing their names. There were Champagnes from Argentina, Cognacs from Spain, and vodka from Israel. The bottom shelf was labelled "doubles". There was just a large white envelope containing a single bottle. In a great understatement, someone had written "1811" on a corner of the envelope. Inside was a second bottle of the 1811 Roi du Rome Cognac.

The labels are now housed in the Cognac alcove along with books and menus.

Wines of Bandol Alcove

The **Bandol region** is world-famous for its rosé wines, which are considered among the best in the world and are predominantly produced from Mourvedre grapes. It received its AOC in 1941. But there are other fine wines produced in the local region such as Côtes de Provence (AOC, 1977) which is made from Carignan, Cinsaut, Grenache, Mourvedre and Tibouren grapes; Coteaux d'Aix-en-Provence (AOC, 1985) and Les Baux-de-Provence (AOC, 1995) made from Grenache, Cinsaut and Mourvedre; Cassis (AOC, 1936) made from Clairette, Marsanne, Ugni Blanc and Sauvignon Blanc; and Coteaux Varois (AOC, 1993) made from Grenache, Cabernet Sauvignon, Cinsaut, Mourvedre, Syrah and Carignan.

Wine has been produced in this region at least since the Greeks settled in Massalia in 600 BC, if not before by indigenous peoples. Romans, Saracens, Carolingians, Holy Roman Empire, the Counts of Toulouse, the Catalans, René I of Naples, House of Savoy, and the Kingdom of Sardinia all contributed their individual wine-making styles and viticulture to this Mediterranean region.

Wine has produced on Île de Bendor's sister island, Les Embiez since 1901 and was separated into AOC Côtes de Provence and Vin de Pays du Var. Domaine Les Embiez produces red, white, and rosé.

The elegant metal and ceramic table between the displays is one of the few remaining on the island of over 100 that graced many of the hotel rooms on the island but disappeared years ago when the rooms were renovated and modernized. This is a classic Provençale style. It was built to last and to remain stable in the highest wind, an essential feature when the mistral arrives.

The Production of Wine Alcove

Modern vermouth is a relatively recent invention. It is wine, fortified in the style created by Arnaud de Ville-Neuve, and flavored with as many as 24 botanicals. Vermouth takes its name from the German word for wormwood—*wermut*—and is an extremely bitter shrub that has been used for thousands of years as a treatment for intestinal worms. The earliest record for wormwood-infused wine we have discovered dates back to 2500 BC in China. By the 1600s wormwood wine was common throughout Europe. Even England's Queen Elizabeth I was known to drink a glass every day. In Holland, *alsom wein* as it was called was very popular.

The Court of Wallenstein in what is now the Czech Republic, declared the 1633 vintage to be particularly good.

Modern vermouth was born in Turin, then the capital of Sardinia, in the 18th century. They produced a dark coloured vermouth that was sweet, balanced, and pleasant to drink. It was normally made from sweet white wine. The colour and part of the flavour came from burnt sugar—caramel.

In the early 19th century, dry vermouth was invented in the south of France, in Marseillan. Today half of the annual chamomile harvest in France is used in vermouth.

There is a wonderful story that a blind monk named Dom Perignon invented Champagne (AOC, 1936). The truth is sparkling wine occurs naturally and had been documented for some time before his birth. Wine bottled in the fall would begin a second fermentation in the bottle or cask in the spring when the weather became warm again reactivating the yeast. It was given names like *"vin diable"*, or *"saute bouchon"*, and winemakers worked hard to get rid of the bubbles before the bottles exploded or blew out their stoppers. Dom Perignon, who was also an accountant in his monastery saw the potential in the bubbles. He found a source of stronger glass and better ways to seal the bottles. When he successfully captured the bubbles, he cried out, "Come quickly, I am drinking stars!"

Champagne should always be opened with care. More people are killed every year by Champagne corks than by poisonous spiders. Each bottle contains millions of bubbles made up of enough carbon dioxide under such pressure that it would fill six bottles in addition to the wine. To compare, a car tire has about 32 psi of pressure. A Champagne bottle has about 95 psi. The world record distance for a Champagne cork popping from a bottle is nearly 60 meters. The director/curators tried to measure the speed of a Champagne cork as it leaves the bottle but, despite repeated attempts, we could not measure a cork's speed with a radar gun.

The proper way to open a Champagne bottle is to place your hand around the neck of the bottle with your thumb on top of the cork. The muselet, the wire cage that holds the cork on the bottle, is opened with six half twists. Then the cork can be held firmly and twisted out of the bottle with a soft pop. The ear's loss is the palate's gain. Opening a bottle gently will keep more bubbles in the glass.

In the 19th century Champagne taps became popular. The tap was driven through the cork without opening the bottle, so that a glass of Champagne could be poured without losing many bubbles from the rest of the wine in the bottle. This also allowed bartenders to add a float of Champagne to the top of a cocktail. Some plaques (the metal disc on top of the cork) were made with a hole in the middle to facilitate tapping. This was much more popular in England than France. This was possibly because the French were less likely to consider opening a bottle of Champagne without finishing it. There are a few different styles of Champagne tap on display here.

Wines of the World Alcove

When **EUVS was built**, Paul Ricard felt one reason to include wines of the world was to show the people of France that someday other countries might produce wines nearly as good as French wines. It seems obvious today, but at the time Canada, Australia, the United States, and other countries were primarily producing very low quality wines. Only a few neighbouring countries, such as Italy, Germany, Portugal, and Spain had a tradition of producing fine wines.

Within a few years, in addition to wine, France was exporting wine experts in great abundance. They were hired everywhere from China to England, Canada to South America. Almost any-where you could find vineyards you would find French wine con-sultants. Thus, great New World wines were born. Today, some truly fine wines are made in Chile and Argentina, California, British Columbia, Australia, Georgia, and even China.

Some of the wines in the collection were gathered by Paul Ricard during his travels, other bottles were brought here by his employees. Many of the wines and spirits in the museum were donated by trade delegations from nations as diverse and China and Cuba, Russia and Chile. When the museum opened, diplo-mats and other dignitaries visited from around the world.

Wines of France Alcove

The **Institut National de l'Origine** et de la Qualité (formerly Institut National des Appellations d'Origine) is the French organization charged with regulating controlled place names. It is part of the Ministry of Agriculture. The first AOC laws were passed in 1936, and most of the classical wines from Bordeaux, Burgundy, Champagne and Rhône had their initial set of AOC regulations before the end of 1937. Today, there are currently over 300 wine AOCs acknowledged in France.

The most recent AOC to be designated occurred in 2009 with the classification of Bugey. Another recent entry is Chaume from the Loire region which was created in 2007. Prior to this, it was part of AOC Coteaux de Layon (before 2003 and again in 2005-2007). In 2003, it was known as AOC Chaume Premier Cru des Coteaux du Layon.

The pupitre de Champagne was originally invented in the early 1800s by the Veuve Clicquot. This A-frame rack is used in the champagne making process. After aging for one and a half to three years, the sediment must be collected for removal. This process, called "remuage", involves rotating each bottle a small amount each day and gradually moved so that the sediment collects in the neck. The *remeur* may rotate by hand up to 17,000 bottles per day.

There you have it: a stroll through a museum that we have grown to love from the first day someone unlocked the door to let us have a peek into Paul Ricard's cathedral to the wine and spirits industry. Three years of sorting, cleaning, discovering, and endlessly feeling humbled by the enormity of the project at hand, we are proud to have the opportunity of introducing you to this very special portion of our lives.

www.ingramcontent.com/pod-product-compliance
Lightning Source LLC
Chambersburg PA
CBHW021053090426
42738CB00006B/322